Copyright © 1998, 2020 by Kristena West

All rights reserved. No part of this publication may be reproduced, distributed, or transmitted in any form or by any means, including photocopying, recording, or other electronic or mechanical methods, without the prior written permission of the publisher, except in the case of brief quotations embodied in critical reviews and certain other noncommercial uses permitted by copyright law. For permission requests, write to the author, addressed "Attention: Permissions " at info@medicinewomenlodge.com

KWest Studios & Medicine Women Lodge
PO BOX 2276
SANTA BARBARA, CA 93120
www.MedicineWomenLodge.com

Ordering Information:
For details, contact info@medicinewomenlodge.com

ISBN: 9798699255580

First Edition

For my father for teaching me dreaming, my mother for her love of the elemental realms, and the great grand adventure of the world of dreams!

Alchemy

The Magical Arts of the Union of Soul©

Dreaming & Shamanic Inner Work for Women & Men

Kristena West M.A.

Introduction

I remember standing on a street corner in bright sunny Santa Barbara, seeing all the busy people bustling to and fro. I turned to my friend and said, "Look, they all have a life. I do not have a life." I have never forgotten that feeling of anxiety and hopelessness.

There's nothing worse than feeling you are on the outside of life looking in. Even worse, in your interior, you're lost and don't know what gifts, if any, you have, or even how to access them.

My father studied the western mystery traditions, and he taught me dream practices that gave me a safe reliable path into the exploration of consciousness. It was through this practice of dreaming, that led me gradually to a new life filled with healing, and inner transformations that shifted my world view and gave me a life filled with meaning and purpose.

Remember Dorothy, when she opened the door after landing in Oz; the world went from black and white to color? That's exactly what happened to me.

It was a dream that told me it was time to start teaching, and a dream that led me to start studying shamanism. By using the tools of the shamanic journey, students gained information, doing weekly work deconstructing the false self, creating transformations, which brought healing in many areas of life.

I was able to go back to school and study depth psychology, gender, council circle training. One of my core questions is, "What makes Art sacred?" This question led me to study for over 30 years with shamans, elders and indigenous ways of knowledge. Dreams gave me a new life path if only I had the curiosity and courage to follow them. I taught the same tools of transformation that helped and gave me a new life. This is the Alchemy work, and the stories of women and men who sat in sacred circle, grinding the stones in their hearts into honey. I have been teaching Alchemy groups since 1990. I wrote the Alchemy book twenty years ago. The work is as relevant today, and will take you into the future. You are being called to a greater life, if you read and *do* the exercises given in this book, and are open to adventure; you will become the Heroine or Hero of your journey.

May we all walk together in Beauty.

Kristena West
Michaelmas- Santa Barbara, California 2020

Sometimes dreams are wiser than waking. - Black Elk

The doors to the world of the wild Self are few but precious. If you have a deep scar, that is a door, if you have an old, old story, that is a door. If you love the sky and the water so much you almost cannot bear it, that is a door. If you yearn for a deeper life, a full life, a sane life, that is a door.
- Clarissa Pinkola Estes

Who in the world am I? Ah, that's the great puzzle.
- Lewis Carroll, Alice in Wonderland

Table of Contents

Chapters
Part One:
Chapter One; Spiritual Emergence the Soul's Awakening
Chapter Two; Alchemy The Great Work; Life Purpose and Destiny
Chapter Three; Accessing Spiritual Realities for Healing and Renewal
Chapter Four; Spiritual Dreamwork Getting Started and Advanced Practices
Chapter Five; Individual & Group Circle Work

Part Two:
Chapter Six; Shamanism, Initiation & Journeywork
Chapter Seven; Soul Essence: Who Am I?
Chapter Eight; Life Purpose: Why Am I Here?
Chapter Nine; Relationships & Sexuality
Chapter Ten; Men's Mysteries: Reconnecting to Soul
Chapter Eleven; Women's Mysteries: Where Did They Go?
Chapter Twelve; The Third Gender: Reconstructing the Cosmic Heart
Chapter Thirteen; The Healing Work of Women & Men
Chapter Fourteen; Creativity the Lost Arts

Chapter One

Spiritual Emergence: The Soul's Awakening

We All Experience "Weird" = Spiritual Events

One night in class I asked the Alchemy group if they had ever experienced something unusual, mystical or metaphysical. The response was surprising. They all started to share some "weird" incidents. Their term, "weird," is code for extraordinary, unusual or mystical phenomena, OBE's, audible voices, dormant healing abilities, clairvoyance, or visions of angels or "others."

When I asked why they were keeping silent about these spiritual events, they replied, "It's too weird, too strange, not normal. Nobody else talks about it either. I don't want to be different." They did not understand that the very thing they were keeping silent about and dismissing was trying to tell them something about their reason for being here and their life purpose.

I gave them the same tools I discovered and had used with good results during my spiritual emergence cycle. Using these techniques, the students were able to understand that there was "something else" infinitely more mysterious coiled deep within them. By using the exercises given within this book, they began to listen to their soul and journey to spiritual realities to gather information and knowledge. This led them into new avenues of thought and challenging adventures, which widened their world-view. By using these different techniques they discovered pathways into soul and spirit--naturally developing a spiritual practice that worked for them. This work also answered questions of life purpose and gave new directions.

❖❖❖

This world we find ourselves in is a mystery play. It is filled with magic, unexplained phenomena, and extraordinary events embedded within our ordinary daily life. Many people have experienced an unusual or unexplainable event, out-of-body or near death experience, a kundalini rising, seen visions or heard voices. Since our western culture does not support direct revelation of the supersensible realms or mystical experiences, we tend not to talk about them.

If we spoke of these experiences more readily in our daily life with our friends and family, it would help normalize this connection we each have. Mostly, these extraordinary unexplainable happenings can cause us distress, anxiety, fear, shock and denial. We might begin to doubt our perceptions, question our discernment, or diminish and negate the mysterious event. On the other hand we may throw caution to the winds and swing into gullibility, interpreting all we perceive as direct revelations from Source and become fanatics, polarized into some form of religious institution.

How we integrate or deal with these "weird" happenings, mystical events, OBE's, visions and voices are the work of all spiritual paths, inner awakenings and soul emergence. I underwent "weird" experiences and dealt with them as many people do. I stuffed them, until something had to give. What I did not know was that I while I was stuffing these "weird" experiences, I was also stuffing my gifts. I did not realize that my spiritual gifts pointed to my life purpose. Eventually, my soul demanded I deal with these "weird events".

If I had been born into an indigenous context, the community would know what was going on with me, as these kinds of "weird" experiences are viewed as the normal unfolding of spiritual purpose. An elder would be appointed to locate a mentor who would have supported me during this process of soul struggle and emergence. Yet, even working alone, what was requested was to pay attention, allow, surrender, investigate, dialogue with, pray and work with the mystical events, and they would point me to my inner unfolding and lead me to discover my life purpose. Who knew? This understanding of how soul works through the body, can be overlooked to our fast moving western culture.

By stuffing and ignoring the insistent voice of my soul I underwent various life crisis. But slowly, by paying attention to the quiet inner voice, tracking my dreams, and processing what was arising in a conscious way, my life transformed and led to healthier, happier and more challenging and satisfying life.

Developing a Spiritual Practice

By developing a spiritual practice you can uncover the mysteries that lie within your soul waiting for recognition. To enter into a spiritual practice takes commitment, perseverance and discipline over the long haul. The rewards however, are great there are treasures, adventures, wisdom and healing gifts that flow from the spiritual beings to us. The purpose of this book is to give you the tools to create a sacred vessel that can contain the power of your soul emergence by:
• Outlining the concept of life crisis as initiation leading into spiritual emergence, followed by integration into a new life path
• Relating personal stories, mystical phenomena and synchronicities that may happen to one and how to integrate them in practical and healthy ways

- Bring information about the Western mystery traditions- with instruction in foundational principles
- How to apply shamanic and psychological techniques for gaining knowledge and understanding in women's and men's spirituality, contemporary life issues, and gender differences
- Outlining how dream work can be developed into a practical spiritual path
- Inform and encourage the importance of continued individual, group and community healing work and rituals

The aim of *Alchemy* is to give people an alchemical workbook they can use to awaken and transform aspects of their soul development. The book is divided into two parts. This first part is an introduction to *The Work of Alchemy*- defining initiation, spiritual emergence, and healing crises as normal results of the soul's expansion. It introduces Western and shamanic traditions and the importance of dreams, and how to recognize spiritual gifts.

The second part is a comprehensive practicum for individual or group work using techniques from these different spiritual and psychological systems aimed at developing a deep understanding of our self in relation to the world around us. The focus is for dialoging with our soul and gaining knowledge in identifying; family systems, relationship patterns, sexual and physical health, creative abilities or blocks, life purpose and destiny.

The *Alchemy* curriculum goes beyond the individual to group work for women and men. It is the first work of it's kind to bring women's and men's spiritual groups together to resolve gender differences while offering a comprehensive practicum for individual or group inner soul work.

A Western Dilemma

Many of us in the West are facing a cultural spiritual crisis. We see the results of this all around us in the rising crime rates, family violence, youth suicides, and use of Prozac as a social norm. Since the advent of our scientific revolution and the scientists' failure to prove that soul exists, God for many has died. We have seen enormous suppression within organized religions that do not stop at cultural annihilation to implement their beliefs. Without risking a gross over-generalization, our society's focus is a highly individualistic and money-oriented one within a mega-industry context. We have been cut adrift to maneuver through life's labyrinth as best we can, relying mainly on ourselves.

Some of us may feel that we are here to do something of merit beyond making money in a high-status job. If we feel this way, we are faced with a dilemma. If our vision goes against the cultural money myth, it requires us to resist the persuasiveness of American marketing tactics that assure us money will grant us happiness, sex, power, and fancy toys.

The other dilemma we may find ourselves in is knowing we want to contribute but not quite knowing what we want to do. This can be extremely painful if we find ourselves at twenty or sixty years of age wondering what our gifts are and how to use them.

The Call to Soul Alignment

The call to align with a higher life purpose can come at any time. And within our American context it can be very hard to hear our call or be rewarded for listening to it. Then, we may ignore it when it comes! So, when many individuals are called to a higher life purpose, they will experience an initiation or a spiritual emergency as a healing crisis. This wake-up call can take many forms: illness, waking visions, deep depression, dreams, voices, or, in the extreme, near-death experiences. Or it may manifest as a trauma, accident, death, divorce, or getting fired from a long-term job. The soul is trying to emerge from within the cocoon of the old life. That old skin is too tight for the soul and must be discarded. This is a critical time when the soul is letting go of outworn patterns and opening to a wider world-view, and the individual needs the support of family, friends, and community.

We seem to have lost touch with the simple things in life, like the natural cycles of nature or farming; preparing the field, sowing the seeds, watering, sprouting, blooming, pruning back, reaping the harvest, then allowing the ground to lie fallow--going into the dormancy of renewal-until the cycle is repeated in it's own time.

By losing touch with the outer cycles of nature we also lose touch with our inner cycles. The American busy-is-best daily format for living wears down the soul forces. The soul longs for other kinds of timing...more circular, slower, dipping, cresting and pouring, it wants to float, hover, sink and absorb, sometimes it wants to rush and rumble...but always it wants depth. If we have lost touch with our souls depth and breadth--we most likely have lost touch with who we really are and what we really want out of life. If our soul is in the process of emergence, and we have lost the awareness of how the soul speaks to us, the time is ripe for a life crisis.

Western Mystery Traditions and Shamanism

I was raised and given foundational training by my parents in the Western mystery tradition of Anthroposophy, a spiritual science founded by the Austrian mystic Rudolf Steiner. Anthroposophy has inherent within it the idea that the soul must awaken and in this process, undergo initiatory experiences. Initiation means to start new—a new beginning or a new

Our Western psychological and medical model often define emotional or physical crisis as neurosis. Many people in the middle of a spiritual emergence will be given suppressive drugs by the medical profession; this drives the spiritual purpose of the crisis or illness deep into the unconscious, stopping the emergence of soul toward a new, healthier reality. Esoteric and indigenous spiritual traditions have a great deal to teach us about life crisis, for they show us how the Western medical model has split soul from body in how we pathologize illness.

Western mystery traditions and indigenous cultures understand illness and healing crises as a normal result of the soul's awakening and expansion—as a spiritual emergence. By using ancient wisdom, we have the opportunity to see that the soul is longing toward wholeness, not further fragmentation. It is imperative for our Western culture to regain some understanding of our esoteric mystery wisdom heritage, which incorporates a spiritual path of power that neither pathologises illness nor stigmatizes the individual undergoing the healing crisis.

Yearning for Spiritual Renewal

As souls, we long for mystery. We long for something to take us out of our lives, change us, shape us, intend us toward something better, something great, toward light, heat, passion, potency and purpose. Although we may desire this adventure into spirit, many of us fight off these experiences, as our egos consider them too threatening.

Joseph Campbell, when speaking of the lure and danger of surrendering into the unconscious, says that these visions and dreams are dangerous.

They are dangerous because they threaten the safe world we have created for our family and ourselves. But the pull to the unconscious worlds also emits a strong lure, a fascinating temptation for us, we desire it and fear it. If we take this tempting bait, we will destroy ourselves and the constructed life we live. Yet the discovery of self, our true nature, will birth a vigorous, adventurous, more expansive whole human with a heart. "That is the lure, the promise and the threat," says Campbell (The Hero with a Thousand Faces, p. 8)

We tend to resist this type of experience, because change is fearful. We will cling to what is known even if it is frustrating, boring, problematic or toxic for us.

What Are the Western Mystery Traditions?

In America, our history of religious socialization and restriction has driven self-realization underground into different movements of spiritual wisdom. The Western mystery traditions are highly diverse wisdom paths, including Theosophy, Anthroposophy, the Gnostics, the Elysian Mysteries, Mystic Christianity, the Rosicrucian Order, Alchemy, the Kabbalah, Hermeticism, Ceremonial Magic, Grail Legends, Greek Myths, Druidism, Wicca,

Paganism, and Free Masonry. It is not the purpose of this book to outline them, but only to note that we do indeed have them at our disposal.

Some of these wisdom traditions are thousands of years old, and found within them are honored pathways into the mysteries of our world. A traveler on these paths will begin to have experiences of a magical, mysterious, or mystical nature. And she or he will begin to dream in a way that can become the vehicle for contacting spiritual beings. Dreamers have been honored in all cultures—even Christian tales are filled with visions, voices, and dreams coming to chosen individuals. My wish for this book is to bring dreaming forward as one of the primary gateways of testing, training, and communicating between the Divine and the individual.

Shamanism

Many people are learning about shamanic or Wiccan systems of spiritual practice. The core concept of both systems is the understanding that everything on this earth is alive, vibrant and inter-connected. By employing different methods to alter consciousness, one can gain access to other realms and gather information, power, protection and healing. Helping spirits will work with us if we are sincerely motivated for spiritual growth. A little understood initiatory doorway into shamanism is through the gates of dreams.

Initiation Finding the Path of Spirit

Initiation means to start. It's a long endless path toward spiritual awareness. Many trials will come to us from within our life events. In most mystery traditions, or indigenous cultures trials or initiations for the neophyte are grueling, life threatening, and painful. Most of the time the person who is being called does not have the slightest idea what is happening.

While the neophyte undergoes these unexplainable events, their outer world will begin to crumble; they may lose their job, home, lover or partner. They may even wonder whether, indeed, they are crazy. These wild and woolly transpersonal experiences begin to exert tremendous pressure on the psyche's solidity, thus stripping the personal ego from the individual whose inner and outer worlds are in chaos. These events can culminate in a transcendent experience that forever changes the participant. This experience rebirths the individual on a deep spiritual and cellular level, bringing much creative change.

Who Gets Initiated?

Initiations are gateways for spirit to enter our lives. Initiations are not limited to shamans or healers. Initiations are rites of passage that happen to one when the soul is ready to expand. We all go through some form of initiation, in a smaller or larger degree, depending on the soul's needs and destiny. In order to awaken to a greater awareness, the soul disassembles personality traits and breaks down our solidified ideologies, which forces us to see our self-delusions and deceptions. Then we have a choice: to continue to live unconsciously or to begin to live authentically. During this process we may experience a transcendent state of consciousness or a healing crisis.

Transpersonal psychologist Stanislav Grof calls initiations "spiritual emergencies" and claims that many of our so-called "pathologies" may be interpreted as the soul searching for transcendence. Grof has spent more than forty years studying and tracking the frontiers of human consciousness. In his classic book, *Spiritual Emergency,* he formulates that spiritual crisis, although highly individual, can be defined in ten major forms.

He outlines them as:

1. The shamanic crisis
2. The awakening of Kundalini
3. Episodes of unitive consciousness (peak experiences)
4. Psychological renewal through return to the center
5. The crisis of psychic opening
6. Past-life experiences
7. Communications with spirit guides and "channeling"

8. Near-death experiences
9. Experiences of close encounters with UFOs
10. Possession states
(pg.13-14)

These transpersonal states can be shattering to the individual undergoing the experience. But if allowed their disruption, expansive unfolding, and if integrated and resolved, they transform us from the inside out. We are reborn and renewed, transformed into a new life.

What Are the Benefits of Spiritual Emergence?

The benefits of undergoing a life-crisis are manifold. When a person successfully navigates through a healing crisis and reassembles themselves, they are healed! Through thee crisis they reclaim their body, giving a deep, centered sense of peace, contentment, groundedness, and connection to source and the Earth. They develop gratitude, compassion, and empathy with which they can help others. Typically they are happy to be alive, having overcome the fear of death and living with an understanding of the sacredness of all things. Many recognize a connection with the spiritual realms that they trust implicitly because they discovered that the real reason they survived their initiation crisis is the love, grace, and compassion of the spirits.

We will go through many types of trials in our lives. Our testing and challenges arise out of life events, inner and outer landscapes, and altered states of consciousness and dreams. Once we have successfully navigated through one such experience, we see the world differently, but this does not mean that life is sweetness and light or that we are on cruise control. My experiences and what I have witnessed in other people's lives show that one initiation prepares the ground for the next one, and so on. We never quit growing. We will reach other plateaus and will need to jump to the next level. But between those initiations are periods of seeding, rooting, growing, and blossoming before we have to contemplate leaping another hurdle.

To know something about a healing crisis is a great help and relief to the person undergoing it (which may be you), as it provides light at the end of the tunnel. If this fits for you, consider getting help from someone who knows about spiritual emergence. Healing crises can be viewed through many lenses: traditional psychology, transpersonal psychology, shamanism, Christianity, Buddhism, spirituality, or western medicine. In the latter case, doctors tend to stop, limit, or halt the crisis through prescribed drugs. It is very important to get compassionate support if you can.

Healing the Split

Every one of us is on this journey into wholeness and the discovery of life purpose. If you are stagnant, frustrated, spinning-out, or floating without direction, you may be stuffing something extraordinary about yourself. You might be sitting on a treasure, your gift for the world.

The Work of Alchemy is to listen and work in co-creation with your soul nature. Each of us is here for a reason. We have come bearing gifts. We need to discover our spiritual gifts, come to an understanding and acceptance of our life purpose and actualize it. In aligning with our purpose, we serve our soul, each other and the earth. The earth needs her children to wake up and remember who they are. It is time.

Chapter Two

Alchemy: The Great Work Life Purpose And Destiny

The journey toward the actualization of our soul-self into wholeness is termed "The Great Work" in Alchemy. Many times in our lives we need to make choices that require leaps from one state of existence into another. This can look like changes in outer forms such as deciding to leave an stagnant career into a more authentic one, going from a married state into being single again, or moving from our hometown into an unknown community. It can also look like transformation in our interior states; rebelliousness into positive focused action, jealousy into self acceptance, self-hatred into self-love, depression into allowance, anger to forgiveness, or illness to health.

These changes always spring from our deep interior self, a shift in our priorities, a quickening of soul, a personal healing. To make these changes either on the interior or exterior levels means that we have to change or transform who we are. How do we make creative change in ourselves? What are the steps of transformation and internal change?

First, we must have the ability to self-reflect, to look deeply into our personality and character and see ourselves with radical honesty--to come to an understanding of our repressed selves, creative abilities, beliefs and behaviors. Second, we have to develop the ability to discern what we as Soul *really* want from what we do not want. Third, we must be willing to surrender, allow, open and commit to our healing process and take the action steps necessary to seed, water, prune back and rebirth our selves with patience, care, honesty and love.

A spiritual-psychological definition of Alchemy is when one allows the self to surrender to a death process of the inflated ego, diving deep into the chaos of the unknown, into the interior darkness and sitting still long enough...until a quickening develops and eventually births a new and transformed personality and character.

The Inner and Outer You

Our journey through the complexities of life centers on our basic desires for a satisfying career, good health, a beloved partner, pleasurable sexuality, joyful creativity, and a fulfilling spiritual practice. Those of us who grew up in Western society may not have one or more of these treasured gifts due, in part, to a loss of connection with our inner spiritual nature.

As we progress through the many stages of life, we are touched to the deepest strata of our emotional being. Our inner emotional field encompasses; loves, hates, conflicts, births, sacrifices, purifications, victories, deaths, losses, and redemptions. Our conflicting emotions, wishes and desires are focused through our career, sexuality, relationship and communication patterns, creativity, wounds and addictions, destiny, and our spiritual practice--or lack of it.

Within many stories is embedded the symbolism of the human battling the "evil" side of his or her personality. Dr. Jekyl and Mr. Hyde is a wonderful analogy of the separation of the "good" and "bad" inside of us. In that story, Mr. Hyde had to be killed off. There is another way to view this duality of internal forces. The Work in Alchemy suggests there is a union for these struggling, opposite forces within the psyche, a synthesis of both our positive and negative poles blended into a powerful integrated authentic self-hood.

The transmutation of old into new means we must melt down our outworn constructed personality into a new or revisoned self. To do this we must die to the old-self in order to be reborn. In simple terms, it means letting go of our ego-driven desires for *Me-First*. We do this by dismembering ourselves, by allowing our self-created false face or masks to dissolve, and then we can re-member ourselves as we truly are and claim our destiny.

Our Beginnings: Coming to Earth Bearing Gifts

To start this journey, we begin with the soul and the purpose of incarnation. We do incarnate for a purpose—we come to the Earth bearing gifts. Each and every one of us is unique, with gifts for the world. Perhaps you have forgotten you have a gift or two tucked carefully within your soul. You do. These gifts can translate into your destiny, life path, or right livelihood. They can translate into what is termed your soul essence: who you are at the core of your being.

Do you remember when you were little and life's potential filled your body with exuberance, and you felt that you could do anything? Absolutely anything? There was so much to choose from, and so little time; which would be the best choice? In your heart of hearts, you felt that you were special, that someday something would happen and a miracle would be around the corner for you alone. Then you would be called to your destiny. You may not have known what it was, but you knew that it would fulfill your deepest desires!

If you haven't manifested your inner calling yet, do not give up hope. There are a number of reasons that may be occluding your path. In our American culture we are not taught that we are unique souls bearing inherent gifts for the Earth. Even if we recognize these gifts within ourselves, we may not be encouraged to develop them—especially if the gifts cannot be designed as "money-makers" or they do not fit the cultural norm for acceptable careers. Parents, society, or financial pressures can turn many of us away from our inherent gifts. We do this to be accepted by our family, friends, community, culture, or religion. In doing so, we lose a part of ourselves—we lose soul.

The Loss of Purpose

In childhood, if we receive the message that who we are is not OK, the first thing we do is a very creative act. We make up somebody who is OK. We create a false-face personality for ourselves. We play the game of "Let's Pretend." In doing this, we push many unique and individual qualities down under our presented surface. We desperately want to fit in, look normal, act like the others, or become invisible. We don't say what we really feel, and this eventually changes to not feeling or not knowing what we really feel. This game becomes real when *we* forget who we are.

This is not a bad thing. We do it to survive, to make it through. We saw our situation for what it was and we adapted. If we had to hide ourselves in the process, so be it. If your parents didn't like the arts, for example, you may have stuffed your burning desire to be a tap dancer. If your family did not like outbursts of emotion, out go the angry retorts and the joyous, rapturous, youthful yowling's. If academia is approved of, there goes bohemian behavior. This is the stuff that births teenage rebellions; teenagers are trying to reclaim what they lost in childhood programming.

Years may pass and we eventually forget that we're playing "Let's Pretend." We simply believe we are who we say we are. We have bought the act. So once we have not honored ourselves or the soul's direction, it is much easier to give ourselves away again and again. After giving away our heart's desire, we are more easily swayed by the group norm, and we can get involved in a career for monetary or status reasons. We may marry someone who is not a match for us. By creating a false-face and giving up our dreams, we lose parts of our soul and forget who we are.

If we lose touch with our soul-selves, we cannot recognize what suits us. Many people go through life without conscious thought about destiny because we are struggling to pay the rent or mortgage, take care of the kids, get our work done. We don't have time anymore to think about what our calling might be. Or perhaps we had some hard knocks and lost faith in ourselves, even if we are engaged in a successful, "chosen" career.

The Search for What We Think We Want

For many of us, something seems to be in the way of our finding the "right" man or woman, the "right" job. We may feel blocked, shut down creatively, or we just haven't had the breaks. Many times we think the problem lies out there with "them." We tend to think if we just met the right person, made the right connection, or had some good luck, we would be much happier. But the news is that the problem usually lies within our own natures. *We* tend to repeat the same patterns by making the same choices in relationships, jobs, sexuality, and creativity that bring to us the same lesson over and over again.

It may look as if life's circumstances, bad luck, or timing is at fault, that something "out there" is doing it to us. Life does present obstacles and challenges. But the world we find ourselves in is created by our choices to act or not act regarding many life decisions. If we are making decisions from a place of our created false-self, we will be asking these kinds of questions:

What *should* I do?
What will be *acceptable?*
What will the *others* think?

These questions are based on fear. If we continue making decisions based on who *we think* we are, then we perpetuate the compromising of our soul-self. We can end up with a tremendous amount of emotional pain, finding ourselves locked into a career path and marriage we hate. In order for us not to feel our confinement, fear, separation, anger, guilt, or shame, we employ great ingenuity in creating diversionary tactics; drugs, sex, alcohol, work, sports, and so on. The behavior patterns we develop in order to avoid our pain are the same ones that keep us from finding our right life path, our beloved, a creative life, health, and a rich inner life with spirit.

Our addictions and other compulsive behaviors reflect our attempts to stuff or shut the gaping hole of hurt. When they create only more pain, separation, and isolation, many of us eventually find our way into psychotherapy, support, or recovery groups. As we struggle with our helplessness, our anger, our betrayals, our fear and tears, we dive in and out of a deep valley of pain. This is an initial step toward developing an internal dialogue with self while identifying patterns within us that hinder, block, or sabotage us. Here is where we open up the dreaded can of worms—the sacred wound.

The Wound Leads to Soul Realignment and Destiny

To identify our sacred wound means to uncover where we lost ourselves, where we split off our soul parts and created a masked persona. This once highly creative act has become a death mask, for underneath we are dying. We are dying because we know we are hiding our worth, our light, and our juiciness, our wildness—our passionate, delectable, true selves—under a disguise. This is our wound, pure and simple. The healing process is a call from soul to realign. In this realignment we get to clear and uproot the negative messages, protections, body and mind armoring, lying, theories, patterns, beliefs, and compulsive behaviors we have habitually engaged in since the beginning of our self-creation play.

As a facilitator and teacher of right-livelihood, I have seen countless people who were already manifested in the world: doctors, artists, contractors, psychologists, and teachers. They all had one thing in common, they were miserable in their jobs. Many of them felt they were called to do something else but could not figure out what it was. Some of the lucky ones knew what they wanted to do, but for some unknown reason, they could not transfer into the other chosen vocation. They had the social, economic, and technical skills necessary, but they couldn't make the shift into their right livelihood.

As you can guess, this caused them great emotional pain. Many of them had done the requisite years of psychotherapy. They worked in the classes on addiction–wound correlation, discovering where they got off track, creating goals, and planning action steps. Despite the group's support, their personal commitment, and daily action plans, many of them were unable to venture beyond what was known and safe toward their chosen destiny. Why couldn't they hold onto their calling to right livelihood? Why couldn't they move forward?

Timing; the soul's timing may be different than what we think we need. Sometimes there is a hidden matter, something of which we are not aware or that has little to do with us, that may be settling outside events into the correct position for us to venture forth.

Some people find out that they are at the beginning of their self-discovery journey. They are just beginning to realize that they do not know who they are. At this part of the journey, focusing on goals like, "What am I here to do?" is premature. Their inner work lies in uncovering the layers of misinformation, hidden dreams, and forgotten childhood qualities and discovering where they lost themselves, identifying what they created as a false persona and why.

Soul loss is another factor. Participants in class who held onto their dreams and knew what they were here to do could not manifest because they lacked the spiritual power to do so. Many of them had lost soul or spiritual power during traumatic life events, internalizing negative messages and the creation of their false personas. What many of them needed was a spiritual healing to bring back that which was pushed out and split off from the soul.

Psychologists say we dissociate during trauma. This is true. From a shamanic point of view, these "soul parts" don't usually come back. This soul loss leaves a hole or a lack within the soul force that we feel very deeply. We develop behaviors to stuff or stop us from feeling the black hole within. Thus begins our inner battle. The wound, the memories, the anger, the despair, the fear, the addictions are denial patterns of the personality in direct struggle with spiritual life and our calling.

Soul Retrieval: Reclaiming Lost Aspects of Self

The wound is where we denied or got diverted from our spiritual path. But psychology, tells us that to identify, feel, and release the pain of our wound is to bring wholeness and healing to our body, mind, and spirit. Yet so many aren't healed even after years of psychological work. Using the shamanic technique of soul retrieval can bring results and individual healing by bringing back spiritual power.

Receiving a soul retrieval can be a primary first step on our healing journey. We have all been through some form of trauma in our lifetime. It takes time to integrate a soul retrieval. But over time, as the power is integrated into the soul life, aspects of the self that have been out of balance begin to realign. This process can be easy and relatively uneventful or it can take conscious effort and intent. The inner work really begins after spiritual healing.

If we don't get our spiritual power back, one of the problems we face is not only repeating painful patterns but also talking about them. Our story is the road into the wound. We tend to repeat our trauma both in outer events and in the stories we tell. If we are unconscious, then we may not understand that the soul is weaving the hero or heroine's journey. Our job is to pay attention and follow the thread into the labyrinth.

There is great power in voicing our wounds as our oral traditions tell us, but there is a shadow side as well. Many of us tell our wound stories as ways of relating. The problem with working our wound story is that many of us identify ourselves as wounded: codependent, sex-addicted, eating-disordered, and alcoholic. This becomes the unconscious identity and life-path--a victim. After a few years sitting in support groups, we rehash our stories again and again, receiving attention and sympathy. We actually are receiving negative attention for our wounds and no support for healing.

Who We Are Intended to Become

I am not advocating the omission of core wound work. It is a foundational step in self-knowledge. But we in the West are inundated with a psychological framework that defines us as victims of our parents, victims of our society, victims of gender, race, and poverty, even victims of wealth.

35

This is a limiting view as it dismisses the spiritual world, previous incarnations, self-responsibility, and healing as an option.

Many people feel that these side roads, mistaken directions, or family wounds have wasted their time, hindering them from going forward and manifesting destiny. This is not so. Your life story is your spiritual path. What else would it be? Your way to God, Goddess or Spirit is through your stories, myths, deceits, and epiphanies. We must honor the soul's timing. But if we want to get on with the purpose of our lives, our destiny, we must face the wounds where we alienated self and go through the fire of our pain to reclaim our lost soul aspects.

We are more than our stories of past hurts, pains, and failures, however. Indigenous wisdom supports this view by saying that in our Western culture we spend too much time looking at our past and not enough time *looking toward who we are intended to become.*

The reason for psychotherapy, self-help, and the diverse kinds of body and soul work is not just the identifying, grieving, and rehashing of our wounds as the talking cure. It is also to hold the container for *what we will do with ourselves once we are healed. Who are We Becoming?*

Life Crisis Viewed as Initiations

For many of us, it takes a life crisis experience to lead us into our healing process. The healing crisis leads you to Who You Are Intended to Become. It is during this crisis initiation we must melt down our bones into soup. Like a butterfly creating a chrysalis, we spin our cocoon, be it our self, marriage, job, or religion. Our patterns, our beliefs, and our constricted social norms—all is melted down in a "breakthrough" experience. When the shell of our old self falls away, we can remember who we are on a soul level. We are reborn of spirit and the world is changed. We look at things differently.

As we travel through the many layers of the healing process, we move into and out of different stages: denial, awareness, grief, anger, acceptance, soul retrieval, and eventually healing. Life crisis can be viewed as initiations into new states of being. The soul will emerge despite our best efforts at enclosure of self. If we do not allow the creativity of our deep self its expression it will create a life-crisis scenario which we cannot avoid. This can look like something that comes at us and envelops us from the outside world; the loss of our job, a marriage that splits apart at the seams, an automobile accident, or death of a loved one. How can we view these crisis in a spiritual context?

The research on *some* of the well documented "poltergeist activity" has been traced to the repressed inner combustion of the psycho-spiritual life within individuals, rather than ghosts or spirits without physical form. The phenomena of flying utensils, moving lights, and things that go "bump in the night" are outward manifestations of huge power and potential within the psyche. This is an interesting idea we can adapt to the eruption of life crisis as spiritual emergence. The erupting forces that cloak themselves in life-crisis scenarios are our repressed true spirit nature that is beckoning. The spirit is knocking. Our inner nature is demanding existence.

Life crisis can take innumerable forms. They can hammer us into an inert mass of confusion, desolation, despair, anger, and denial. We can refuse the fracturing and dissolution of our built-up ego personality--which will bring us further pain, or we can let go, allow, and surrender into the process--*feeling* our way through our fears, denials, and pain.

The resolution of our crisis is our healing journey. Going into the fire of transmutation takes guts, courage and grit. It takes commitment to an inner intimacy accompanied by opening to spiritual power and protection.

The Gifts of Dreams During Life Crisis

Many crisis experiences can come not only in our life events but also in visions or dreams. Your dreams will help show you the way through the fire into your cauldron of transformation by the dream scenarios you encounter. The fluidity of the spiritual worlds held within the context of your "dream" is a perfect container to map who you are and where you are in your life path.

Your dreams will support and guide you, giving you hope when you least expect it, in the dark night of the soul. Working with your dreams will give you daily information, messages, warnings, and health guidelines. Dreams will show you your false face or shadow self. Dreams will give you a safe arena in which you can identify, confront, and battle your enemies, be they abusers, addictions, or your shadow nature.

We can awaken to our calling by kindling the inner potentialities through the use of dreamwork as a connecting link to the spiritual worlds and their inhabitants. Dreams can and do initiate us into states of awareness, recognition and resolution regarding our life issues. We can even receive healing of our physical, mental and emotional bodies within the dream context.

The Great Secret of Initiation

Once in a dream, a spirit asked me, "Do you want to know the Great Secret of Initiation?" I replied with a gasp, "Yes!" It whispered, "Before, During, and After." On awakening, I smiled. How simple! Yet, this is the essence of initiation.

In our *Before* state we are either in a fully manifested arena of life that has reached its peak or a closed chrysalis state, unconscious. Then our initiation crisis envelops us, this is the *During* state. It is *During* these crisis initiations that the closed door of spirit opens and divine insight, guidance or grace may be given. After this experience we are not who we used to being--we are in the *After* state--we are different, new, reborn, and, we cannot go back.

The first few minutes of a butterfly emerging out of its chrysalis is a critical time. The butterfly must be in a protected environment as it must unfold its wings, stretch them out, and vibrate them into fully functional wings capable of soaring on the wind's up-drafts. The same is true for the soul. Coming out the other side of an initiation crisis is a fragile time. We need to stay in a protected state where we are as safe and peaceful as possible. We have been shaken up, dismembered, and, like the Scarecrow in *The Wizard of Oz,* there may be some of us all over the place. Take the time to regroup, reform, and assimilate your new psyche form. This is very important. It may take some months or even years before you have an understanding of who you are in relation to this new world.

The Gifts of Resolving a Life Crisis

After resolving your life crisis, you will see and feel the world in a different way than you did previously. This includes how you view people, what you say, how you say it, what you wish for, and what you don't. Initiation lines us up with our authentic soul-self. Reassembling will affect all areas of your life. You will see where you are out of balance sexually, creatively, and spiritually, as well as in communication skills, compulsive behaviors, career, health, physical habits, and intimate relationships.

Aligning yourself authentically does take time; you have to let go of the old patterns and instill new ones. But it will be a natural unfolding, a natural reorganization of who you are because it is based on authentic selfhood. Initiation is a rebirth, and you will have the spiritual power and vitality available to implement the healthy and creative changes so you can get on with the life you intend and live your dreams.

The Importance of Ritual Work for Core Integration

Another necessary adjunct to the healing process is ritual work for anchored and integrated soul stabilization. Creating and enacting different rituals formulated to our story, calling on spiritual forces for assistance or focused as a personal healing is one of the most powerful and important tools available. Rituals can be used at the beginning, in the middle, at the final stages of a life crisis journey, or in a closure ceremony.

Ritual is not just a symbolic forum for the soul to release, contact, or provide a rites of passage for it's journey. The ritual context is an opportunity to work in conjunction with potent spiritual forces or principalities for the individual. We must realize that the world is filled with potent forces waiting for our call to assist us in our evolution, healing and soul actualization. Spiritual beings will bring in enormous power within our rituals and lift us into altered states of consciousness whereby we can open to receiving a greater density of vibrational spiritual healing energy.

The acceptance and reliance on spiritual realities to provide the electricity for our ritual empowerment is our first step in results oriented ritual work. This can challenge our early childhood "religious" socialization, much of which we may have left behind us--but even our twelve-step support programs are firmly founded on spiritual principles. We are realizing we cannot do this inner work alone.

Numerous stories abound about the help from spiritual realities in the dark night of soul crisis--this points to the idea that we are being watched, helped and supported through these tough and problematic passages. Ritual is intended to transform the issue, problem or wound into connection to certain spiritual forces and potentialities--that will assist creatively within the individual's physical body, mental awareness, and emotional field. Ritual work in alliance with spirit forces will help heal our wound.

Our wound is meant to be healed. We are meant to be whole. Our wound must be identified, felt, expressed--safely and authentically--resolved, and eventually forgiven. Then our attention should naturally move away from our wound and its associated self-absorption toward the world and what we are to give to it. In healing our sacred wound, we uncover our spiritual treasure, our spiritual gifts. Spiritual gifts define our character, our calling, our destiny and right livelihood, and are meant to be used in the service of others.

Right Livelihood:

An Inner Alignment of Soul with it's Spiritual Purpose

Focusing specifically on finding our right livelihood does not mean that we will become a Hollywood starlet, a president of a company, or a billionaire by fifty, although for some people that may be their destiny. It is not about making X amount of dollars so we can afford lots of toys, cars, and the model husband or wife. We are not here to make more and more money and equate that with amounting to something. We are not here to continue a superficial lifestyle of me, me, me, and mine.

• **We are here to hone our gifts into a destiny that will give us the satisfaction of knowing we developed our calling into an offering to the world.**

Right livelihood is an inner alignment of soul with its higher purpose, and for many this is the gradual unfolding of the heart for service to humanity. This can mean that we are asked to use all our capacities, and more, to stretch to our greatest potential and formulate a career where our soul-self can give back. For many this may mean a career change, but it may not. We may find we have had the perfect occupation or career all along and feel blessed with it. This includes that most sacred thing, being a mother or a father.

We do not necessarily need to change our occupation in life to come into an inner alignment of soul. Many times our life path is developing the *character* of soul, which is a "being" quality, not a "doing" occupation. By bringing ourselves into alignment with our higher purpose we will bring into balance what is repressed, suppressed, and depressed into the psyche. This transformation is a change in essence that comes from the inside out. The underlying reason for all initiatory experiences is to bring a cosmic awareness into being within our inner life, so that we may teach and live that consciousness outside of ourselves in our daily activities. The questions we ask ourselves now sound more like this:

What am I *passionate* about?
What do I *want* to do?
Will it be *worthwhile*?
Will it *benefit* myself and others?

These questions are based on a solid sense of self-worth and self-esteem; they are not based in fear. These are the types of questions that spring directly from your source. They envision a life path or right livelihood, one in connection with soul and others. One way to pinpoint authentic life paths are the feelings of excitement, joy, and happiness--but an equally powerful way-depending on which way we are wired-is the life path that fills us with great resistance and fear. Following those emotional threads will lead you to your calling.

Spiritual Emergence

Although our personalities may not be aware of it, as soul, we long for initiation. The soul wishes manifestation—the unfolding of our heart, mind, and body in harmony with the Earth. The soul does not wish to hide itself under misrepresentations. It wishes to shine forth and blossom into full flower.

Many of us are unaware of the greatness of our soul's worth and where it is heading, so we limit ourselves to a narrow confine in our life arenas. Also we may be scared to move in directions that feel uncomfortable or new to us. We may feel the frustration and pain of hanging in there with a life style we can't stand, yet we are unable to let go of it long enough to see what rises up within our soul life.

Because our Western culture does not hold the container for rites-of-passage rituals, shamanic healings, or initiatory tests, we come upon them unaware; or, rather, they come upon us who are unaware. Life does initiate us. We will be broken open. This is necessary for our souls' growth and our expansion and creative potential. Nevertheless this is usually an unpleasant business because we cling to what we know and what we feel comfortable with, even if we are hurting or miserable.

The spiritual world knows our greater destiny and sees how our wounds block our life purpose. The spirits are filled with compassion for us and so orchestrate opportunities for our healing by presenting us with many choices until, faced with our repeated refusals to listen and take heed, they kick our butts into an initiatory crisis.

It can take an initiation crisis to move us out of our control and limitation paradigm-- to crack our hearts open. Initiations many times are looked back on, as grace in action, as blessings, as miracles that lifted us to a greater level of living and loving. The key is to look underneath the present scenario to the spiritual lesson that is calling to you. Following that spiritual Call is the start of the alchemical process of transmutation; of turning your dross into pure gold.

Listen. What is calling to you at this time in your life?

Chapter Three

The Power of Ritual; Accessing Spiritual Realities

for Healing and Renewal

We in the West are aware that we are in a major spiritual crisis. Although many of us are self-reliant, independent and either self or college educated, yet for all that, we live lives of isolation and quiet desperation. We are disconnected from the earth, each other and our inner most self, our soul. This malaise translates out into numerous and varied symptoms of restlessness, unbalance, illness, anger, fear, depression and ultimately destructive behaviors toward self and others. This progressed way of non-relation implodes within us and we can tumble into a "dark night of soul."

But we long for connection. We long to relate to others. We long to relate to our community. We also long to be able to relate to ourselves. We need to discover who we are and penetrate into our spiritual nature. How can we begin the journey home to ourselves? What tools or techniques can help us revitalize our heart and develop connection to a deep-rooted sense of spirit?

One of our greatest tasks in this new millennium is to reconnect with the spiritual beings as a *living reality*. How can we revision our religious, indigenous, mystical and esoteric revelations into a working cognitive construct for ourselves? One of the questions that arises out of our souls is, "How can we touch and interact with the spiritual beings?"

As we look around the world at different cultural holy rites and within our western religious traditions we discover that what is enacted cross culturally are rituals. As humans we have an inherent predisposition of soul to enact ceremonies and rituals in order to bring us into realignment experientially with the spiritual realities. Through the use of Ritual as a potent symbolically charged ceremony we move spirit through our bodies instead of intellectualizing it in theory.

Ritual Frees the Deep Self

Ritual frees our deep self that lifts us to higher and loftier levels of energy. But that is not all. When moving into sacred space we alert the beings that hover near us in the *Other Worlds*, and when we call on them with sacred intention they move into alignment with us, and through us within the ritual context.

The importance of ritual has long been recognized within the church as well. The seven rituals of the Catholic faith were used as high magical ceremonies to transmute the energies of the spiritual realities through the priests (and the nuns as receptors) into the congregation. If the participants opened to the resonance's being brought through, they were lifted on the wings of angels and higher forces poured into them. Much of the knowledge behind these rituals have been lost, as the ceremonies are typically enacted in a rote way.

Although we find many of these rituals throughout western religions, so many people have left institutionalized religions for more expansive and inclusive routes to God or Goddess. Therefore ritual is the work must be remembered, and integrated into viable path working for us in a practical manner. It is up to us as individuals to endow our daily life with the power of rituals that once the church supplied for us.

In order to this we must educate ourselves in ritual work, the nature and scope of spiritual realities, the discipline and ethical modalities of magical practices and ceremonies. Also, we must develop a community in which to do this work.

Groups and Circles

Circles and groups invite us to step out of our isolation and drop our masks of self-reliance and self-absorption and into intimate communion with others. The conscious raising groups of the sixties gave us the format of circle work-and in that work we witnessed the depth, agony, grief, relief, and healing work of "listening" and being "listened to." We realized that this is what we had lost-communion within the circle-the compassion, humanity, and kindness that flows naturally from one human to another within the sacred space.

Circle work is one of the easiest ways in which to connect to others in deep and transformative ways-hence the popularity of the women and men's movement. With the addition of spiritual intention the dynamics and depth of the group process is expanded to include the other worlds. We must reopen the hidden gateways to the spirits.

Creating Personal Rituals

A gateway to touch spirit is to ritualize our wounds, hopes, grief's, funerals, births, weddings, and rites of passages within a collective context. Personal rituals can be improvised, dreamt, designed, spontaneously created for anything in our life we wish to clarify, heal, express, intend, or ask of the Source, God or Goddess, Great Spirit-- how ever we define it.

It is essential that we be seen and recognized by others within a community or group context for what we have endured and gone through. This is how we actually heal and move beyond the habitual retelling of our wound stories. We arc meant to move beyond them and into the self-actualizing of our souls, to embrace our destiny. In order to embrace our destiny we must actually heal from our wounds. This means our *ritual has to work*. In order for our rituals to work we must be in co-creation with the spiritual orders. *They*, the spiritual beings, empower the ritual. We do all we can to line up our intention, hold our focus, and open up our soul forces to engage the spiritual hierarchies and focus their power through the ritual itself.

The most important thing about going into ritual space is the sincerity of our heart's intention toward spirits. When we enact a ritual we are entering into sacred space in order to speak with, bring into balance, heal, or to request something from the universe.

Creating Ritual Space

Creating ritual space is done by delineating ordinary space from non-ordinary space. Creating ritual space can be done by building altars of earth, air, fire or water-which ever element will help the ritual work you are undertaking. Creating and building your altar is a way to focus the intention and your energy of your ritual.
Casting the Circle: One of the simplest ways of creating sacred space is casting a circle around the ritual space. Circles can be cast with symbols, salt, tobacco, sage, or with intention. Rituals can be done inside or outside-but I encourage you to work outside with the forces of nature and the land spirits if you possibly can.

Adornment: to Delight the Eye. Ritual space should be adorned to lift it from the ordinary to the extra-ordinary. Sculptures, candles, beautiful cloths, flowers, incenses, chalices, blades, ancestor shrines, talismans, all enhance the visual stimulus to a higher frequency.

Closing the Circle: We must cast or delineate our sacred space, open and start the ritual, enact the ritual and ground and close the ritual space. Opening and closing the gateways is critically important discipline and must be carried out. When we open and call on the forces of the spirits, they move in and around us, when we close we thank them, perhaps gift them and ask them to depart from the circle. This keeps us healthy, and the boundaries sharp and clean to ordinary and non-ordinary states of consciousness.

The Power of Rituals

Rituals bring us into a charged atmosphere, of sacred space and into alignment with the unseen so we can see and listen with our hearts. When we enter our ritual time can stretch and drop into a trance or altered state of consciousness. At these times we are more open to receiving ideas, healings, creative directions that spring "out of "no where" and directly into our heads and hearts.

Rituals can be done for endings, beginnings, transitions, divorce, marriages, new jobs, births, deaths, earth ceremonies, and pagan rites. Rituals can be done on your personal altar simply because you wish to connect with spiritual reality.

Creating personal rituals on an ongoing basis will build the foundation stone of inner soul development. As you go deeper into the use of ritual you will learn about power: gathering power, holding power and focusing power through the ritual itself. Knowing how to use power wisely is one of the components of competent ritual work.

Gathering Power and the Right Use of Intention

Ritual ideas are easy to come up with as rituals arise spontaneously out of our wounds, hearts and life problems. The reason rituals work however are not because of the excellence of the ritual or the tools used within the ritual itself. The reason ritual works is because of the combination of the sincerity of our heart's and the power of the spiritual beings. When we enact a ritual we are in essence going through empowered motions—motions that are empowered by the spirits.

Learning how to gather power with a sincere heart and to concentrate or focus while enacting the ritual is what is asked of you as the human part of the ritual. The spirits will move into the ritual, the object or the song if those prerequisites are in place. Then your ritual will be spirit-powered or spiritually empowered and will bring results, healing or a lifting of the obstacle—whatever the intention of the ritual space.

Ways to gather power are many: movement, dancing, singing, drumming, rattling, meditating, concentrating, breath work, and yoga. The easiest ways to access power are usually through singing, dancing and drumming or music. Rattles and drums are easy to move and pack up for nature ceremonies or healing rituals outside your home. The more people in the ritual the more power available as a focused fulcrum of intent. But solitary ritual work will bring results—but it is up to you to raise the power within your body-temple and enact the ritual with a pure heart and concentrated intention.

Power moves through the body differently some people feel hot to sweating or cold and chilling, some people move directly into ecstasy and some people feel expansive. Some people feel breath or air touching them when there is no open window or air source—all these are examples of power or spirits moving into the physical body.

As you get proficient with these methods, singing a simple song can be sufficient to cover your body with chills or heat or for you to feel ecstatic. Learning a power song is a simple and easy way to gather power. Some people discover they are natural singers and spontaneously start singing before a ritual or a healing--the melody and or words just "come" to them. This practice opens up our hearts, and throats and brings us into interior alignment, and opens us up as temples to house power and spiritual beings.

Songs as Living Prayers

Songs are prayers used to call the helping spirits, which bring the needed power to you for ritual to work. A song can be simple; vowels, singsong, or words. If it is given to you by spirit it is filled with the spirits power. You can use this for your ritual, healing work, before important meetings, to draw power and protection to you. This is a foundational element in your spiritual practice.

Rattle or drum for five or ten minutes until you feel power moving into your body. Then sit quietly for a ten-minute meditation to ask for a spirit song. Just listen quietly until you hear a vowel, words or a melody starting inside your heart. Then start humming and singing it until it flows through you. Use this song with a drum or a rattle to call in your helping spirits. Make sure you do this many times until you are very proficient and it flows.

Chapter Four

Spiritual Dreamwork

Getting Started and Advanced Practices

Dreaming is one of the most easily available ancient techniques of acquiring spiritual wisdom known to us. Dreamwork serves the soul, turning it toward the light, toward health, wholeness, and individual destiny in alliance with our spiritual nature. Developing your personal dreamwork is a natural way to begin or to augment any spiritual practice.

Dreaming has long been the doorway through which artists, creatives, healers, thinkers, inventors, and philosophers have ventured to Other Realities, and brought back gifts for our earth. You can use applied dreamwork as a way to gather information on your personal life, guidance in life path, for insight and direction, and to uncover creative abilities.

Applied dreamwork as a spiritual path will present you with all the challenges that a truly profound teacher or adept would, including adventures, tasks to complete, challenges, tests, and the work of consciously integrating the shadow. Dreams can bring much need guidance when we feel all interior channels are closed. For instance, when you experience a dark night of the soul, having done everything you could to help yourself, your dreamwork provides the possibility of a healing dream or divine intervention.

There are many books outlining applied dreamwork without a spiritual format. However the Alchemy text is based on the premise that we live in a spiritual universe surrounded by spiritual beings-the aim of this book is to give tools, techniques and information that will help you make direct connection with the divine however *you* define that. This includes meeting and working with your teachers, guides, angels, and power animals.

Advancing on the Dream Path

People who apply themselves to their dreams in a spiritual context will begin to have more advanced dream guidance, tests and adventures. As you progress and successfully complete tasks and tests given to you in your life and dream events, you can be initiated into realms of spiritual knowledge, wisdom, and power to be used in the service of our community and the earth.

Many women and men, as well as shamans have been given divine gifts, ecstatic experiences and healing powers directly through the dream. This is available to the sincere seeker. Spiritual dreamwork however has a built-in flaw proof system of initiation--only those who have honed their character, moral qualities and who have struggled with their ego will be given these types of gifts. What follows are some sample questions you might want ask as pointers to focus on in journaling your dreamwork. All these questions and more can be answered by paying attention and working with your dreams. Listening to, working with and taking the action implied within your dream guidance will give you results in daily life.

The Basics
How do I begin to remember, map, and interpret my dreams?
How does applied dreamwork give results in my daily life, and what are the benefits?
How does dreamwork relate to my current life events or problems?
How do I know what the dreams are telling me in relation to my complex life questions?

Healing the Sacred Wound
How do I use my dream guidance to help me through a habitual problem or addiction?
Can I actually receive a healing from an addiction or compulsive habit in my dreams?
How can dreamwork help me in relation to my unconscious sabotage patterns?

How do I heal early childhood trauma through dreamwork?

Health

How can dreamwork help me with my health?
Will dreaming give me guidance I can trust?
Will it warn me in *advance* of any disease? Can I receive a healing?

Sexuality

Can dreamwork help me to find my Beloved?
Can dreamwork help me with my children, my husband or wife?
Can it help enhance or heal my sexuality? How?
Can I have a dream lover?

Life Purpose & Destiny

What are my spiritual gifts? Will dreamwork identify them?
Can dreams help move me toward my destiny?
How do I translate my spiritual gifts into a life path?
What does my destiny have to do with the greater common good?

Creativity

How can dreaming help me to awaken my creativity?
Can dreamwork help me with a creative problem?
Can my dreams point me in the direction of a creative path?

Spirituality

Can I count on my dream teachers in times of spiritual need?

Can I have a mystical experience? Meet God/Goddess? What effect will it have on me?

Can I undergo initiations into more advanced personal work through dream-work?

Friends and Allies in Spiritual Reality

Our earth is filled with creatures of earth, air, fire, and water as well as trees, stones, plants, crystals, and animals. Similarly, there are numerous beings from diverse spiritual systems on the inner planes. These are not outmoded psychic forces or inner soul symbols, neither are they a new-age discovery. They are aware, evolving, living realities, endowed with vast spiritual powers. When you begin the task of dreaming and ask to be taught this ancient art and craft, you will send a signal into the spiritual worlds. That signal will be answered. The dream becomes the vehicle through which your soul speaks to divine sources.

We all have teachers though many of us are unaware of them. We are never alone, despite how we might feel. We are helped, guided, and prodded by our unseen angels or spirits many times during the day and night. As humans we enter into relationship with the higher worlds through contact with supernatural beings, with the Creator/Creatrix at the apex. If we can separate this construct from different religious dogma, we can use it as a frame of reference for touching the ineffable through dreaming.

As you record your dreams you will begin to identify certain dream teachers who will come to you over and over. Sometimes they may not show you the same face, but you will notice the same energy showing up in either a male, female, animal, stone, or tree form. These teachers have immense patience supported with inordinate amounts of good humor. They will send you "punny" dreams—dreams with double meanings, laced with humor. If we can laugh at ourselves, we are halfway home. As you get used to working with your dream teachers, you will begin to develop trust and dedication, a sense of purpose and anticipation, and an acceptance that they have tremendous good will toward you.

Here is a basic system to lay out your dream practice for cultivating dreamwork. Whether you are a beginner or a long-time enthusiast of dreaming, it is always helpful to review the basic steps.

Crafting Your Dreamwork

If your life is like mine, approaching dream work means simple practicality is easiest, with a sacred intention holding the container. So the first thing to do is to intend to remember your dreams and ask to be taught in your dreams. If you do this with sincerity, the dream teachers will know that you are willing to pay attention to them. They send dreams every night regardless of our sacred intent, but I find that with *sincere intention* over time comes true dreaming.

To learn the language of your dreaming you must honor and keep track of your dreams. This means developing your memory and writing the dreams in a spiral notebook or journal. On the front of each new journal I write with a big, black marking pen the starting date, and at the end of the notebook, I write the closing date. Don't forget to put the year.

Keep your journal, a penlight, and a pen or pencil by your bed. In my journal I note the full date and then write about my day's activities, goals, worries, thoughts, what I am reading, and my daily dreams. As an artist I will sketch a small drawing from my dreams in the corner of the page. Sometimes this dream art catches the deeper meaning of the dream better than a long explanation.

Another thing that holds magic is naming the dream. After writing the dream, come up with a few words for the title and write them at the top of your dream description. Dream titles—like Caged Eagle, Dead Kittens, Dragon Eggs, New Houses, Eight Months Pregnant—can help us drop quickly into the dream's emotion and content.

Here are some basic dreamwork tips:
• Every night upon going to sleep, declare your sacred intention to remember your dreams, and ask to be taught within your dreams.
• Buy a spiral-bound five subject college notebook or blank journal. Label it with the month, day, and year of the first entry you make. When the book is full, enter the last entry's date, too.
• Keep a penlight and pen or pencil by your bed within easy reach.
• Have a cup of mugwort tea before going to bed. Mugwort is a dreaming herb. You can also try tucking a small pouch or pillow filled with mugwort under your pillow to court dreams.
• Try to wake up naturally, without an alarm clock. If that doesn't work for you, set a clock radio to wake you to low-volume classical music (or other gentle music without words). Give yourself at least five or ten minutes before you have to get up.
• On awakening, don't move! Just lay in bed quietly. Moving your body activates motor centers in your brain that take you out of the imaginal realm of dreaming, and the dream will wisp away. Keep your eyes closed and stay in the same position in which you awoke.
Allow yourself to stay in that state between dreaming and consciousness. Follow the trails of your dreams. If you

remember the first one, they often unravel backward and you can track the previous one.

If you cannot remember what you dreamt, ask yourself, "Person, place, or thing?" to help jog your memory.

- Write down your dream(s), all the details you can remember: the smells, tastes, sights, sounds, textures. Was it day or night in the dream? Were there period costumes? Were you in another century or country? What was the emotional quality of the scene? Notice whether there were any puns, plays on words, or words with double meanings. Any visual innuendoes? If what you remember is just a snippet, that is good, too. Write it down.
- Sketch a scene from your dream to help capture an important image.
- Jot down a title and be sure to note the full date of the dream.

Western Mystery Tradition Dream Training

My father was a devout student of the western mystery traditions. He started my dream practice when I was a child. He told me, "Sleep is the little sister to death," and that every night we leave our bodies and fly to other realms. These nightly travels are taken in another body which is usually termed the "dream-body" or "astral" body.

You can train yourself to become conscious of the fact that your awareness is not limited to your physical form-to become awake in your dream. The first time this happens and you view your body lying in bed asleep, many people have one of two experiences--great joy or great fear. The joy is attached to the fact that they realize there is more to life than they previously thought. The fear is usually the fear of death or the unknown-with a mad scramble to try to re-enter the body.

My father told me, that just as by day I went to school, by night I went to another kind of school, a school of higher learning. He said I could access that school anytime if I needed help with a problem later in life. He said that many creative people have gone to this library or school and brought back ingenious designs or information that will help the planet. To help me get to this other school at night, he gave me this exercise to help me learn to leave the body. He told me to do it every night while I waited for sleep. This is a great exercise-try it.

While lying in bed before going to sleep, see or imagine yourself floating out of your body to the ceiling, then through the roof and up into the cloudy sky until you rest on a cloud with the Milky Way and planets circling around. Then drift into sleep.

By following his instruction and the exercises given I learned to leave my body in sleep and see the hidden worlds with my own eyes. I also understood that mystical realities are hidden from people until they reach a certain moral and ethical resonance. I endeavored to work on myself and use my body as a science laboratory to test the validity of dreaming as a viable portal into other realms. I also wanted to leave my body consciously at death, and this was another extremely strong incentive toward learning the art and craft of dreaming. When I got older, my father gave me this dreaming assignment-it is to facilitate crossing over the threshold of sleep consciously, seamlessly.

When lying in bed at night try to keep your attention at your third eye, the point between the eyebrows, and not let it drop.

~Three Main Categories of Dreams~

Potato, Reflection, & Big Dreams

Dad outlined the framework for categorizing dreams. "There are three kinds of dreams," he said, "potato dreams, reflection dreams, and big dreams."

- Potato dreams occur when you eat too much rich food for dinner. Heavy foods, late at night, make for noncohesive dreaming; he suggested not to pay too much attention to potato dreams.

- Reflection dreams are just that: your psyche or soul reflects on your day and reworks some of your decisions, makes suggestions, or judges your actions. Dad said that to avoid reflection dreams I should go over my day backward every night while lying in bed waiting for sleep. I should think about where I lost my temper, where I may have hurt someone's feelings, where I could have made another decision to bring more balance into a situation.

- Big dreams are, of course, spirit dreams, medicine dreams, true dreams, or shamanic dreams, the ones that change your life. For me, they are usually lucid and fraught with portent and awe. They feel power-filled, a direct message from the world of spirit, and one never forgets them. They can be clear messages or directions, prophetic in nature, and sometimes healings are given in them.

Dream Incubation: Asking the Spirits for a Dream

I asked my father how does one get an answer to a question or life problem from a dream. He replied with the Three-Day Prayer.

If you have a question that you would like to ask the spirits, condense it into a single question as simple and to the point as possible. Then when lying in bed, simply pray your question to the spirits, asking that they send you a dream answer. You are to do this with enthusiasm, focused intent, and sincerity.

Dad said, "It takes a while for your spirit body to hear you, and so you have to ask the question three nights in a row. When you ask the question, you put your will force and longing (like praying) into the question. On the third night, you will have your answer."

"What if on the third night I do not receive the answer?" I asked.

He said the answer might be kept hidden for a reason or I might need to try harder. If I tried for a period of time, say, two weeks, and still no answer, then I should let it go and trust the spirits will tell me when and if I am ready. This is a reliable method that works.

Categorizing Your Dreams

The next step upon receiving a dream, is to learn how to interpret their meaning. Dreams can be literal, metaphorical, symbolic, shamanic, and archetypal. Many layers of meanings can be held within one simple short dream. Learning to interpret a dream can feel overwhelming. A suggestion before you begin to interpret your dream is categorize it. Place it in a context that works for you, this will give you information you can use later for interpretation.

Try reading over your past dreams and look at the elements in the dreams. You'll discover they can be broken down into basic categories. Many dreams cover multiple areas, so count them in as many categories as appear helpful. This will help you begin to see the themes your soul is working on in the dreamtime.

The categories I suggest below overlap in places, and every category can be broken down into subcategories. For instance, mother-father can be feminine-masculine, wife-husband, anima-animus, Goddess-God, and queen-king--depending on your cognitive context. Dying can be divided into; drowning, being shot, dying in sleep, dying in war, being knifed in the back, having a heart attack, falling off a precipice, killing yourself, being killed by someone else. You can make up your own categories to add to these.

Context: What Is It?
- Father/Mother • Childhood/Teenager • Family • School
- Sexuality/Lovers • Anima/Animus • Right Livelihood • Health
- Creativity • Destruction • Nightmares/Crisis • Sacred Wound
- Spirituality • Initiation • Prophesy • Shadow/Projection
- Birth/Death/Dying • Earth/Global • Community/Nation • Cultural Context

The Earth Landscape: Where Is It Happening?

- Woods/City • Attic/Inside House/Basement
- Bedroom/Kitchen/Bathroom
- Backyard/Front Yard • Work/Home/Doctor's Office
- church • Childhood House • Adult House • Another Country/Planet
- Train/Plane • Automobile • School Bus
- Space Travel • Desert/Beach • Doors/Gates
- Stormy • Cloudy/Clear • Bright/Dark
- Water/Fire/Flood • Natural Disaster • Cold/Hot

The Time Zone: What Time Is It?

- Day/Night • Dawn/Dusk/Sunset • Current Time
- Another Century • Waking • Sleeping • Present/Past/Future
- New/Old • Watches/Alarms • Period Clothing • Wedding/Funeral
- Breakfast/Dinner • Marriage/Divorce • Saying Hello • Saying Good-bye • Work/Play

The Action: What Am I Doing? What's Happening to Me or the Dream Characters?

- Birthing/Dying • Sacrificing/Killing • Having Sex
- Manipulating • Dominating/Submitting • Vomiting
- Dealing with Broken Toilets • Helping/Ignoring
- Seeing/Can't See • Hearing/Can't Hear • Talking/Can't Talk
- Running/Can't Run

The Emotional Quality: What Am I Feeling or Sensing?
- Anger • Laughter • Fear • Threat • Terror • Confusion
- Violence • Happiness • Pleasure • Sensuality • Devotion• Orgasm • Joy • Optimism • Emotionless • Stuck • Fat/Thin
- Exhaustion • Frustration • Neediness • Arrogance • Powerful
- Weakness • Hatred • Competence • Health • Sickness • Anxiety • Sadness • Grief

This should give you plenty of ideas for categorizing your dreams, the symbols and life events they incorporate. Dreams typically will have one or two of these categories as the most powerful or potent; often there will be a quality or feeling that you can't shake. Put that into the dream title. At the end of your dream description, jot-down a few words describing the lingering elements and work on them during the day. Here's a sample description of a dream like many I had while attending the university.

1/30/95   Climbing the Mountain

I am climbing to the top of a huge mountain. The air is cold, crisp, and the sun is brightly shining. The terrain is rocky, with a narrow dirt road winding far away to the top. The trail is well marked and clear of brush. I am halfway up. I am carrying water and a backpack—it is not too heavy. I'm wearing jeans and good shoes, all current attire. I see no animals or other surroundings, only this mountain fills my view. I am very tired. The top of the mountain, where I am going and where I can rest, seems very far away. I am discouraged but, as I look behind me, I am surprised to see that I have come farther than I thought. I am more than halfway there! This rejuvenates me, and I continue with renewed vigor. Interpretation: I am overwhelmed with studies and am currently working seven days a week. But I am also very happy with my progress and although tired I am re-amping to continue through till graduation. I like the fact that there are no storms or clouds on the horizon.... I feel good about my goal, bright and sunny. I have to be careful though, as I am tired. I'll see if I can take some time off to rest soon.

Note: signifies end of dream and beginning of my notes to myself.

    Now that you have some ideas about how to write down your dream descriptions, you will also want to learn how to interpret them. Not all dreams are as straightforward as "Climbing the Mountain" which is a metaphorical dream. Many of them are not literal but are metaphorical, appearing in symbolic format. Then, you may ask, how do you interpret your dreams? How do you follow the thin smoke trails upon awaking? How do you know which dream to pay attention to and which comes from your dinner? How do get a handle on a metaphor? Practice, practice, and practice. Pay attention. Pay attention to the dream, your connection (or lack of) to Spirit, your ego, your work, your mood, your sexual life, your creativity, your family, the Earth. All these come into play in relation to the interpretation of a dream.

Dream Interpretation

To learn the art and craft of dreaming you must learn to interpret your dreams correctly—correctly for *you,* that is. By listening to the nightly conversations you are having with the spirits, your life will forever be changed. Interpreting your dreams is a lifetime task, so be easy with yourself. Dreams are like Chinese boxes: one meaning nests within another.

Dreaming is your direct experience of the Divine, and only you are qualified to interpret your dreaming. Dreaming is a self-empowerment tool: it is yours to hone, to make mistakes with, to validate, to use, or to ignore. Dreams come to you specifically, using your symbols, myths, and cultural archetypes, the movies you've watched and the books you've read. The dream teachers know you better than you do, for they know your unconscious and the secret wishes of your heart. Given that, how could anyone else interpret your dreams?

Other people, for example, participants in a dream group, may help you and give you much needed prompting in a certain direction, but only you can have the gut knowing of, "Yes! That is what it means to me!" Dream groups are sources of profound learning for individuals, and if you can find one-or start one-I highly recommend joining a dream group long-term.

If we learn to *interpret* and *use* the knowledge of our nightly adventures, we will wake up to a new life and spirit. There are many viable dream systems and techniques to chose from and adapt according to your dream interpretation needs: Jungian, Gestalt, Shamanic, Tibetan, Dream Yoga, and Senoi, to name a few.

In the West, we have been told that others hold the secret key to knowing: the church, a guru, this or that teacher, professor, or psychologist. But this is not true. We have a divine source within us that will teach, heal, guide, and help us on a daily basis, free of charge! So, if we chose to develop the discipline to look within ourselves for our own answers, we will be rewarded with dream gifts for the soul.

Over time, you will begin to understand the language and metaphors your dream teachers are using. When this happens there follows, usually, a feeling of utter delight, as it is "proof" that you are in contact with spiritual beings that are indeed talking with you. This will give you added emphasis to keep your attention on your dreaming.

To use dreaming for guidance you must commit to it, and dedicate your morning time to writing down your dreams and mulling them over during the day. Over time as you work with the spiritually imbued symbols and guidance, you will deepen and deepen in your trust and reliance of the process, and the support you receive will build your foundation for dreaming as a spiritual path.

After learning to remember, write down, draw, and interpret your dreamwork, the next question is obviously, "What do I do with it?" Sit with it. Allow the dream to work within you. It comes with its own power embedded in the metaphors and symbols. That power will emanate into your inner soul forces and work within you. After the fun of following the clues in the dream, you will arrive at an understanding, and then you can apply the knowledge, hints, and directions to your daily life.

Application of Dream Information

Most systems of dream work when done with sincerity over time will bring about deep inner soul transformation. This is the essence of spiritual practice. We just mapped a foundational dream practice; recall, recording, categorizing and interpreting of dreams. After journaling, categorizing, interpreting our dreams comes the last task, that is the application process itself--taking what is given in metaphor, scenes, symbols, language, direction, hints and applying them to your life situations. If we do not move our dream messages outward in creative action, we are just information gatherers-collectors. We must use the dream guidance, hints and nudges and apply the action steps necessary for our personal growth and transformation.

Our nightly dreams will be; indicators of physical health and well being, warnings or guidelines, creativity pointers, relationship patterns, repressed shadow traits, symbols of our emotional nature, sexual health updates, and life path directions. All dreams can be journeyed back into by using a shamanic journey, creative imaging, meditation, artwork or journaling. These additional modes of re-entry will bring back forgotten dream information, deeper imagery or point out additional avenues of reflection and action.

- If you are ill or your physical body is depleted in some particular vitamin or mineral you may receive dreams about food. Many times just before I wake up, some food will be floating before my inner eye; bananas, broccoli, oranges or lemons. The next step is to *eat it*.

You may be shown what food is causing you anxiety, sleeplessness, or even harm to your body. You might be shown piles of empty alcohol bottles, or a tape measure wrapped around too much food, or a skull and cross bones over an image of food, pills or liquid.

- If you are working on your love relationship or to improve your sexuality you will have many dreams showing your shadow self in relationship, your communication skills-or lack of them, you may act out your healthy pleasuring or be shown your sexual inhibitions--all in your nightly dream theater.

The task is to take the dream images, dialogue with them, paint them, struggle with them, and work with them until you understand what they are asking of you. Then do the next step as they indicate which might be--join a support group, or inform yourself with self-help books, get a therapist, take a dance class--move the energy of the dream into action steps.

• If you are working on sexual abuse issues, you will be given many ideas, messages and dream scenarios that outline, augment, and potentialize your healing work in that arena. Many times this will include repeating dreams and nightmares meant to "wake the person up" to unconscious or unseen work. Using the dream guidance will help propel you toward wholeness. This kind of work is usually long term and done over years.

Many unique methods of healing can be done within this context in the dreamtime. One woman I know, called Louise astral projected in her dream to confront her mother's spirit-also out of body. Louise knew her mother could not lie as she was in spirit form--Louise found out pertinent information and the truth of her molestation; this dream information was validated by Louise's sister later that year. Astral projecting (conscious awareness and the energy to perform a given task) within a dream is a gift that can be developed through applied dream practice.

• You may see signal lights that you can apply directly to a current event in your life. Seeing a Red Stop Light will usually mean, "Stop what you are doing! Stop! In the direction you are heading!" A Yellow Light will mean, "Use extreme caution! Stop, and consider before progressing further. or maybe Danger!!" A Green Light is, "Go! It's Clear and Easy Progress! Just Do It!" Take the advice or warning and apply it your life issues.

• If you are focused on finding a beloved to marry, you can use dream incubations or prayers to ask assistance in receiving dreams that tell you time-lines, possibilities, what sabotage patterns you may be running to block this alliance, to ask to review your relationship patterns, communication dynamics, sexual health and your true intentions in this matter. This is potent work as it touches on the triggers within us that are loaded with energetic information; our deepest desires and greatest fears-intimacy, communication, sharing, love and sex.

- If you have suffered a loss; a divorce, death, or miscarriage-you can ask for dreams that will support your healing process. Many times the spirits of the departed visit frequently working with the individual until their issues are resolved.

After a divorce many people discover on looking back that their dreams were informing, warning and pointing out guidance for years before the divorce became an option. You can ask for dreams that will help you resolve and come to understanding about what happened, how to deal with it, where your blocks are, and further healing work needed.

The Spiritual Gifts Given Within a Dream

Taking a look at religious, indigenous, shamanic, and western mystery traditions we find that many gifts are given directly through the gates of the dream. One of the primary doorways into shamanism is the gate of dreaming. Many shamans' are gifted with healing powers by the spirits from the "other side." One of the reasons some people are given these "spirit" gifts over others, is that the person is dedicated to their spirit path, disciplined in their practice and is willing to use the gifts for the benefit of all.

Some of these gifts are the ability to heal others, clairvoyant sight, audition, prophecy, kundalini awakening, out-of-body experiences, astral projection, merging with animals or teachers as allies, spirit marriages, the gift of plant spirit allies as an herbalist or healer, knowing who is going to die, psychopomp work, the power to deposes spirits, magical practices, rituals, sacred art.

One night I asked for a definition between a lucid dream and a shamanic dream. That night in a dream a spirit voice stated, " A lucid dream is the ability to control your dream events. A shamanic dream you are given a gift directly from the spirits."

Audition: the Voice of a Spirit

Audition or the hearing of a spirit voice typically occurs as one is going into the sleep state or just upon awakening. " The voice is usually described as androgynous, forceful, expressionless, impersonal. Rudolf Steiner calls this "hearing with our souls" in his foundational book, *How to Know Higher Worlds.* He goes on to state, " ...then a new sense of hearing comes to life in the soul. The soul becomes capable of hearing "words" from the spiritual world that are not expressed in outer tones and cannot be heard by physical ears. Perception of the "inner word" awakens. Truths are gradually revealed to us out of the spiritual world. We hear ourselves spoken to spiritually. (Pg.47, 48)

Audition is a direct link-up to the Divine. In the mystic traditions audition is the experience of hearing a voice imbued with power and irrefutable authority. If listened to it can bring illumination and transformation. Audition is one of the first gifts on the mystic path, but many people other than mystics have these experiences--artists, inventors, writer's, and scientists--usually at a critical turning point.

I have heard such a voice I was a child. It has directed me to expand, change course, to take the next step. I consider it a profound gift of guidance and take it's counsel without fail. When I was at the University studying psychology as a major, I heard this voice thunder, "Start Writing!" I looked over the other majors and saw that with a communications major I would have to take many writing classes. I switched majors and learned the skills of writing. I could not guess at that time I would be writing for newspaper and magazine articles, much less a book.

Plant Spirit Allies

Some people are given the knowledge of how to use plants to heal and become either herbalists or plant spirit healers. Specific plant spirits will often visit a person in a dream showing it's essential healing powers; how to distill the root, stalk or flower's healing essence, and how much of it to administer. Using this type of gift, with its power to cure is why many of our European and American medicine women (and men) were labeled "witches" and murdered. This is one of the main ways that we lost our shamanic arts. None-the-less, these gifts will never be lost as long as their are students of the sacred dream there are spirits who are willing to teach.

Sacred Art

Many people are given direct training in sacred arts. They are shown how to design, make and empower ritual art objects. When one is given a dream art image, shown what materials to use and how to empower it, they become sacred artisans. These kinds of tools, masks, or ceremonial art will carry the power of the spirits and it's maker. When I decided I was going to start a business making spirit dolls, I was trained for years on all the aspects of doll making and empowerment. I was shown how to make armatures, bodies, wig, costumes and rituals to empower the doll-every night in my dreams.

I have an artist friend who receives fully detailed shamanic art projects. He sees these just before he actually awakens--they come as visions. He then finds and creates exactly what he saw in the vision. He has pictures, costumes, and ritual regalia all over his studio. The interesting thing is, he knows nothing about shamanism! But he will do what he is given in dreams. One full figure he made covered in leaves stands in his studio--when he finished this piece-his dog started howling at it. That is spirit filled art!

I receive art or ritual tools to make for myself, others, or to use in my healing practice. If the spirits give you a dream ceremonial art piece, my advice is to make it and use it. If you do so, you show respect and gratitude to the spirit world and your willingness to work in co-creation with them.

Power Animals and Totem Spirits

We can receive alliances with the animal spirits or totems through the gates of dreams. Power animals are our allies who come to help and assist us in power, protection, sexuality, luck and joy and to reconnect us to our bodies and the earth.

On the first night of my women's circle I have the students do a power animal retrieval for each other. One woman, named Rachel, received a wolf as a totem spirit. Rachel was somewhat leery of this power animal, but equally curious and honored. She had her doubts about the reliability of her partner's ability to really retrieve an animal power for her the first time out.

That night she had a dream. In the dream she is watching herself on a lonely cliff top, standing overlooking the night sky. From up behind her she sees the shadow of a giant wolf stalking her. She watches the wolf come up behind her unaware self...the wolf raises itself on it's hind legs and puts his two front paws on Rachel's shoulders. Rachel instantaneously was inside her body feeling the weight of the wolf's paws, and feeling the hot breath panting against her neck.

The dream alliance with the male wolf was a profound synchronicity that helped Rachel open to the reality of spirit allies. As she continued to work with her totem spirit, she was given many other "synchronistic" events, gifts and dream wisdom teachings.

Psychopomp Dreaming:

Helping the Spirits of the Departed

One of the most important lessons in dreamwork is overcoming the fear of death. To do this, the dream teachers will give you every opportunity to experience many layers regarding the mystery of death. This is not something one learns right away, in a dream or two. Usually this takes repeated, long-term dreamwork, until the soul realizes that it is spirit and the body is only a house dropped into during the daytime.

One of the ways to teach about death is to help people who are leaving their Earthly bodies through this transitional phase. Occasionally, in dreaming, I would help people who are "dead" and stuck in personal belief systems to have a different understanding of the Divine and the afterlife. To help the dying cross over, or to assist the spirits of the recently dead to find their way, is called psychopomp work.

Spirit Messages from the Departed

Making contact with departed loved ones is easy to do in the dreamtime. Since we are out of our bodies at night, our spirits can receive information or go to different areas of learning. A few years ago an acquaintance of mine, whom I will call Stephanie, telephoned me. She was flipped out.

A very dear friend of hers named Rob had died by a freak accident. Rob came into her dreamtime begging her to give his family a message. He was very upset. Rob told her he had tried to contact his family and his girlfriend but they seemed to be too distressed to be aware of him. He relayed that his family was cutting his girlfriend out of his monetary inheritance because he did not make a will. He asked Stephanie to contact his family and tell them his wishes regarding his money, which was to split it equally between the family and his girlfriend. Stephanie, who knew about my work, asked me what to do. Although she felt very strongly that her departed friend had made contact with her, she was uncomfortable about approaching the family with a dream message.

The situation was volatile. It is up to the person who received the dream message to make the decision on what to do with it. Stephanie, after checking in with herself, decided it was not her place to interfere. But she watched the situation and much to her amazement the family did an about-face and shifted their position concerning the girlfriend. Both parties came to an amicable agreement. Stephanie felt that Rob was able to get his wishes across to the hearts of those he loved.

Example of Applying a Prophetic Dream

One of the gifts given within the dream is the gift of prophecy; dreams that come as a warning in order to wake us up to potential threat and to give us other options. I have worked with numerous people who will dream the next day's events the night before, but do not understand the importance of the gift being given to them or how to use it.

Within my private practice I will receive dreams of my clients who come to me for shamanic healing or counseling. Not long ago I awoke with a disturbing dream of my client, who I will call Susan, with whom I had an appointment that Tuesday morning. I dreamt,

She was killed in a car accident, on a trip to France. I was hovering above the accident and to the side, I saw she was wearing a red dress, in the front seat with seat belt on--dead.

I had to journey to the land of the dead to find her. The dream changed and I said to her ex-husband who had come to see me, "I just saw her last week."

These precise details-the red dress, trip to France and the statement, "I just saw her last week" places it in time and underlines the importance or criticalness of the information. I work with all my dreams literally first (a shamanic interpretation) before metaphorical or psychological interpretations. When I met with Susan, I told her I had a dream of her and asked if she wanted to hear it. She said, yes.

I told her the entire dream without editing and when I got to the part of "I saw you with your head laying against the steering wheel with the seat belt on wearing a red dress- and you were dead." When I got the part of the dream my body did a full-body blow with what I call truth bumps- which tell me spirits are around. She held out her arms and she was covered with them too.

Here's the facts that Susan related after the dream sharing: she was booked on a flight to Germany via Paris (with an opportunity for a few days lay over there), leaving town in two days, on Thursday evening. She tells me that two or three days previous to our meeting, she had a surge of extreme nausea and when she "checked in" with herself she got the clear directive "Not to leave town."

Although she knew this had to do with canceling her flight to Europe, she had bought the ticket six months previously and would lose the plane fare. She told me another synchronicity; she was in Los Angeles a few weeks prior to our appointment and got a quick vision of seeing herself dead from a traffic accident. This, she related, "Never happens to me." She had the distinct impression to leave Los Angeles and come home, which she did.

We all know how difficult it is to listen to that still small voice within us. But, the final piece for her was she had just bought a new red dress for her trip to Europe!! We used our time together for her to process her feelings about her intuition and my dream. We did shamanic work together and she realized that she was given plenty of interior and clear warning herself. She understood that because of her strong will and ordinary reality details and pressures of receiving no refund, telling her friends and family she was not coming, that she was just ignoring the "advisory committee."

Susan did not get on that plane to France on Thursday night, so we will never put the prophecy to the test. The questions of would the accident have happened may remain, but the only question we dealt with was, was it worth it to find out?

As a dream practitioner questions arise: do I share the dream or not? In Susan's case what if I had not been trained in dream work, would I have ignored it? The next question I ask myself is, what if I chose not to share it and Susan did in fact die? Could I live with that? Prophetic dreams come to us as gifts, but not all dreams are prophetic and we must be able to discern the difference between a normal "ordinary" dream and a prophetic dream. When we can discern the difference, it may be hard to act upon the information given within a dream.

This kind of prophetic dream information is volatile and needs to be handled extremely delicately. As a shamanic practitioner and a dreamer I am required to have discernment and know when to share a dream and when not to. If I share the dream, I must do so with integrity and without instilling fear into the client. To frame it in such a way that it is held in a sacred vessel, but without dramatizing it, and to give the client the space to make up their own mind, through their own inner work.

A Shamanic Dream Healing

In some shamanic dreams, one receives a healing within the dream itself. One of my habits is having a glass of wine with dinner. Although I have used alcohol during times of great stress in unhealthy ways when I lost my brother and mother. Regarding this, I had a dream and was given direct dream guidance, "To do the advanced dream work practices I was attempting, I should not drink--or only on rare occasions." Plain and simple. Direct advice from the spiritual realms.

I began to pray to spirits for a healing. Six weeks of hard praying later, I came down with a terrible infection in my throat. My throat was covered in blisters that went all the way down my esophagus. I could hardly swallow. Excruciating. The throat infection was intense with spiking fevers, chills, and sweats. The third night of this illness I had a dream. (the mysterious number 3 in fairy tales)

I am in a bar with my friends. We are having a great time dancing, laughing, and whooping it up. My friend comes up to me and says, "Come on, Kristena, let's go to another bar and stay out all night!" I look at my watch and say, "You know, I start an advanced training in the shamanic arts tomorrow and I have to get up early and prepare for it." Just then, I look up and see a frightening sight--out of the crowd comes a single figure, a Frankenstein! The creature is lumbering straight toward me! He is tall, large, and squarish. The air becomes thick with threat. He does not take his staring eyes off me. His face is ghastly ashen, his eyelids do not blink, and his eyes are rimmed with multicolored circles spinning round them. He looks mad, stark raving mad!

I awoke terrified, heart pounding, gasping for breath, darting my eyes around my darkened room, clutching my sweat-drenched blankets. From that night on, I did not drink again. Simple as that. It was as if I never had the habit at all. Confronting the spirit of alcohol in the dreamtime allowed me to "see truly" what I was in dialogue with. Seeing with spirit eyes bypasses the ego structure and pierces our soul. The *willingness* to confront our "demons" or addictions, be they alcohol, smoking, over-eating, sex, shopping, or drugs, is the necessary key to healing.

Tree Spirits

Another form of shamanic dreaming is when the spirits of the Earth come to you, the dreamer, and merge with you. When they do this they are allying themselves with you, giving the gift of presence. Then you have an affinity with them and can call on them for help. Earth, trees, rocks, bushes, plants, water, mountains, air, and fire, all are alive with an abiding presence or over-soul. For instance, the night before I started a new class, I asked for help from spirit, to do and teach what was asked of me. That night after falling asleep;

I left my body and was flying around my house. I flew into the living room where I hold my classes, and the oak floor merged with me. I was held inside of the floor and the spirit of the oak tree rocked me gently. This was an indescribably beautiful experience. I felt as if I were being cradled by a loving, nurturing presence. The spirit of the oak was still alive inside the cut and hammered floorboards, and it responded to my prayer. When I sat in circle on the oak floor, I knew that the oak was in alignment with my work and was helping not only me but also the students who were sitting on it.

Dream Lovers

Dream lovers or spirit lovers deserve at least a book by themselves. Some people go to their spirit lover every night in the dreamtime. I knew a woman who had a husband and two children whom she visited every evening. Upon falling asleep she would go to her spirit husband and they would lead a life together for the six to eight hours she was asleep here on Earth. This went on for years. She enjoyed all the pleasures of love, child-rearing, and family life with her spirit family.

A Tree Spirit as the Beloved

Many of our ancient stories talk of times when spirits walked abroad and mythical, magical creatures were an everyday reality. Many of these legends and fairy tales gathered from all over the world speak of the heart-breaking love between a mortal and a spirit. Spirit lovers are extraordinary beings that exist today. One way to meet them is through dreaming. The dreamtime is the playground for the spirits, where our souls can intermingle with the Divine.

Years ago I was living at a house that was built around a magnificent oak tree. I lived there for three years and grew to love this tree. One night it dreamed me.

I am standing in front of the oak tree, admiring it, when suddenly a beautiful man with dark, long hair and green eyes emerges out of the oak tree, smiling. I jump back in great surprise. A tree spirit! He is grinning as if he enjoys this surprise. He laughs delightedly. He is handsome, with exquisite features, He comes up very close to me, the energy between us sparking, and I can see his face is covered in intricate spiraling patterns of purple and green, moving lines of force. Looking into his sparkling green eyes, my soul is utterly known to him and the connection is beyond anything I have ever experienced. I woke to hear my own ragged sobbing.

These experiences are intensely personal. The information, knowledge and love of the spirits is given directly into the soul forces which bypass our constructed rational of reality and how we view the worlds. It bypasses our ego orientation. When the soul is in direct contact with mighty Nature Spirits or beings of the Spiritual worlds, we "know" we are perceiving spiritual realities and in this transfer we are profoundly and irreversibly changed. When you have encounters with these beings you will pass the gates and enter what is called in our myths-the fairy realms or the hidden kingdoms of our universe. Spirits, if they claim you, will continue their association and offer help when needed. A few years after meeting the oak tree spirit I dreamt I was in a place of healing.

I was in a white room with a couple of figures who I knew to be the healers. They had me get up on a table. I lye down and then they put dried oak leaves in black, mulchy earth on my stomach, like a poultice.

When I awoke I knew I should do as the dream instructed, even though I had no stomach upset. I went to a local park and brought back a bag of fallen oak leaves in black mulchy earth. I simmered them in water and made a poultice for my stomach. Later, I had a dream of oak-leaf fairies fluttering just above my hands. I was singing an oak-leaf song to them.

In giving me the blessing of seeing and meeting the Oak spirit, I received a power song. With this song of the oak leaf fairies, they have given me the gift of a magical incantation, or a song that calls the oak leaf fairies to my aid. I can use this in my healing practice--as the Oak has blessed me with a shamanic alliance. These gifts were given me, not because I pursued them but because I love the Oak spirits. The nature spirits know our intent and will gift us if we are sincere. All these "rules" for working with the nature spirits are embedded within our fairy tales, creation myths and legends.

Dream Arrogance

In developing our dreamwork in a spiritual context there may be times where we feel we deserve a higher level of dreams or gifts. Years ago, I invested an inordinate amount of time over three years in intense dream training. I got arrogant. Here is a dream event from that time.

I am in my room, and the dream people come marching out of my closet. They are dressed in ordinary and boring clothes. I get angry. I have read so many other people's reports of beautiful dreams, and mine seem so plain in comparison that I yell at my dream actors, "STOP! Get back inside that closet and don't come out until you are dressed appropriately!" The first row of dream actors stops cold, and the second row bumps into the first. The third row trips over the second row and pandemonium results. They trip over each other to withdraw from my anger, scrambling back into the closet.

I was laughing when I awoke, but later I was also ashamed of myself. I thought about this dream many times and realized what lay underneath my discomfort. I wanted to see spirit in reality. I wanted to see the glorious reality of the Other Worlds through my dreams, and I was impatient. I saw this impatience arise in my dream life as a disgust of plain seeing. I allowed this hidden desire to work within my psyche consciously. Then I had a dream a few weeks later that pointed out the universe's decision regarding my wish.

I am on the Starship Enterprise. We are in uncharted territory. I am very excited, filled with joy. Suddenly my contact lenses pop out of my eyes. I can't find them, and I am distraught! I ask for help to find my contacts so I can see clearly. Captain Kirk comes to me and says that if they give back my contacts so I can see clearly what space I am traveling through, my eyes would bug out of my head. He shows me this by bugging out his own eyes from his head on springy coils, while he is explaining. I am extremely disappointed, yet I understand that he is the captain of the vessel and has my best interests at heart. His experience in these matters is vaster than mine, so I must accept his decision.

    Because I did not want to know what the dream was telling me, I couldn't figure it out for a week or two. I am sure you realized immediately what it said. Denial is a strong companion of inner work that points out ego-oriented shadow material; our egos do not want to be challenged in that way. I was unwilling to be told I was not strong, trained, mature, or able enough to see clearly the interstellar travel I was doing in my spirit body. Which is exactly what the dream was telling me. These two dreams together served to give me a warning: I was not as advanced as I thought, and I needed to wait until the captain of my vessel deigned I could see without impunity.

Spirit Visitations

While you do the exercises within this book or if you are using the alchemy exercises within a group format, pay special attention to the dreams that come through at this time as they may contain a wealth of information. Doing The Work will stir up unconscious abilities, healing gifts, clairvoyance and dream guidance, directions, hints, and true dreams.

By becoming aware of the presence of spirits within our dream time we will also open up to meeting with spirits during our daily life. Over time, we can open to a constant feeling of contact, friendship and guidance with our teachers and animal helpers. This helps us to normalize being touched, gifted or guided by the spiritual realities.

Chapter Five

Doing the Work: Individual and Group Circle Work

The Alchemy Work

In Alchemy the coursework included within this book is called The Great Work. Within *Alchemy* there are numerous examples and exercises that will open your soul to the forces and higher learning offered by the spiritual beings. It is the beginning of a voyage of deep transformational soul work for both women and men. And it is the work of a lifetime. One cannot do The Work and be healed in a single session or group cycle.

The exercises in this book, taken from my Alchemy class, are meant to be used as a holistic forum for spiritual work. The critical factor of self-empowerment found within the practices; dreamwork, shamanic journeywork, and Western mystery techniques—provides a foundation for connecting the individual to the spiritual worlds by paths of direct revelation. This connection develops over time through the commitment and intention of the practitioner. Part Two is compiled in such a way that you can begin the coursework by yourself or within a group.

Cautionary Suggestions

I hope many people who read this book will be called to the experiential journeys with alchemical work using the suggestions given here. I provide these exercises with some precautionary suggestions. If you find that painful information or memories arise or if you are in the midst of an initiatory crisis, I encourage you to get support. That support might include working with a practitioner in one or more of the many forms of alternative healing techniques. It also might include in-depth work with a psychotherapist. First find out what the therapist uses as their "frame of reference" for spiritual emergence. If they use a rigid model in which they may pathologize your experiences and prescribe medication as easily as a medical doctor would, this could halt your process of emerging. There are many highly trained transpersonal therapists and alternative medical caregivers to explore. Find someone who works for you.

Working in Groups

In my class, men and women do these exercises together in a group format. If you'd prefer to work with a group rather than individually, you can use the Alchemy coursework for women-only groups and men-only groups—or groups of men and women together. Using the coursework within the context of a committed group brings one out of isolation and helps one develop a sense of community, love, and connection to others. If you use my Alchemy format, I ask you to stay true to the intention of the work: to bring spiritual knowledge into all the topics covered using the techniques of direct revelation given within the text.

Leaders vs. Leaderless Group Format

Groups can be run with or without an ongoing leader. In groups facilitated by a leadership role, it would be important that you have had good results in your shamanic journeying skills and have a ground of understanding and contact with your dream messengers. This is necessary as you will have to answer the normal questions about the journeywork process.

Leaderless groups are co-run by everyone. There are no designated leaders—the group is committed to equality among all members. Or the group could have rotating leaders, so each person takes a turn weekly or monthly as the leader of the moment. This facilitates the leadership skills of all involved and helps bring forward those who tend to be invisible. All voices will be heard. In leaderless groups, no money should change hands. You can use the work in the chapters of this book for weekly meetings and come up with additional journey questions of your own.

I know that people who wish to use this material for group work will have good intentions. But since this work can, and does, facilitate deep movement, the raising of shadow material, and perhaps mystical phenomena, it is imperative that ethics and leadership skills be addressed, even in leaderless groups. In group work each participant brings with them personal stories, spiritual gifts, ways of relating, communication skills or problems, and shadow material. The possibilities for healing are multiplied within a group context, and so are the interrelationship problems that can arise.

I myself would not have started teaching without the "voice of spirit" telling me to do so. Teaching this level of spiritual work requires a deep connection to spiritual realities; authentic leadership skills; ethical and moral boundaries; the development of character; and the knowledge of group dynamics, communication skills, one's own inner shadow, and how shadow works in relation to spiritual emergence and initiatory crisis.

My background includes some forty years in the container of Western mystery traditions, along with character development, applied dreamwork, and mystical experiences. I also trained as a facilitator of right livelihood for more than two years, did years of varied circle work, received ordination as a minister, and earned degrees in fine arts, communications, and studied psychotherapy. In addition to my ongoing shamanic training directly with the spiritual worlds, I trained with the Foundation for Shamanic Studies for five years. I did my personal emotional, physical, and spiritual release work through transpersonal psychotherapy and alternative healing modalities, including shamanism.

I have seen many groups led by people with little or no training in basic group dynamics, communication skills, or shadow work. This can backfire on the facilitator and the group, providing little authentic healing for anyone. If you are drawn to facilitating group work, you should be receiving good results from your journeys and dreams, develop or expand a solid understanding of professional ethics, group dynamics, mediation, counseling skills, communication skills, and shamanic work. But most importantly, you must have compassionate empathy and a loving heart.

For Group Leaders, Therapists, Teachers, and Facilitators

For those of you already working in the fields of counseling, teaching, or healing who want to incorporate the Alchemy work professionally, there are some guidelines I suggest. The primary tools given in this book are self-empowerment tools for participants and for you as well. All people do the work together; in this way it is non-hierarchical. Everyone is responsible for gathering information. Under no circumstances do you interpret the knowledge that others receive. The Alchemy work is spiritual work, and everyone is working with their own spiritual teachers and power animals. The group participants handle their own information and sharing. They are being taken care of by their spiritual teachers. You do not take care of them. As a facilitator you are there to hold the container, but do not profess your own views on the participants.

Resolving Conflict

Within a group conflicts will arise. In order for the spiritual work to continue, conflicts must be addressed and resolved, whether or not there is a facilitator—otherwise healing will not occur. If the group is polarized with shadow projections or conflicts, then spiritual work will not be successful.

For leaderless groups I suggest the problem be worked on directly within the group, lovingly and with care. Everyone learns many important lessons in the resolving of conflict. When the group successfully resolves a conflict the entire group dynamic will go deeper into intimacy. Conflicts are signposts or nexus points that the group is on the edge of deep space. Many times conflict is the resistance factor to deeper work. The key to resolving conflict is to hear both sides, without blame or shame and come to a resolution that everyone can agree to. In leaderless groups I encourage you to address the conflict in sacred space and deal with it lovingly.

For Alchemy groups lead by a facilitator, you must have the communication skills and spiritual authenticity to hold the group's energy for the release of shadow that will happen for individuals within this curriculum. In order for healing to happen, shadow must be recognized, identified, and re-channeled properly. Since participants sometimes project their shadows onto the facilitator, you must have the ability to mirror, hold, and redirect that projection toward healing. In order to do this you must have intellectual knowledge of projection and transference, the empathy and ability to understand an individual's shadow power needs.

Circle Agreements

In order to help get groups lined up with spiritual intent, I will outline the agreements I use to hold circles. This information has come through years of study plus the trial and error of experience. Participants in my groups make the following agreements with everyone in the group.

1. I agree to respect people of all genders and sexual preferences, to refrain from derogatory comments, and to

honor the people of this Earth in heart, word, and deed while in group.

2.   All that I share and emotionally release within this circle will be released with the intention of healing for myself and all my ancestors. I am not sending this energy to anyone; the circle will transform it.

The Circle Format

I hold weekly meetings that are three hours in length. We open the circle by calling in the spirits by singing power songs, dancing (if there is enough room), drumming, and rattling. Drop into this fully. This creates the sacred space and aligns the group. The three hour class format gives the group about an hour to work on the topic up for discussion and two 15 minute journeys, sharing, and a break. People in the circle share from their hearts what is up with them regarding the topic. Then we journey, writing down the details and sharing them as desired. No one has to share the details of their journeys—for some the journeys are deeply personal and intimate. But people should be encouraged to share enough to keep their energy in the group. At Closing thank the spirits for coming and open the circle.

Using a Talking Stick

Many groups use the ancient tradition of the talking stick. When one person is sharing they hold the talking stick, which can be an object like a smooth stone, a carved piece of wood with sacred symbols, or a totem fetish. Then when they're finished talking, they pass the talking stick to the next person or set it in the center of the circle for someone else to pick up. These are the agreements that hold the container for personal sharing that I use. Agreements set up sacred space and spell out how we will honor each other. When someone is speaking and holding the talking stick, the following council rules apply.

Speak from your heart and be brief. Remember, you don't have to say everything, and don't rehearse what you're going to say.

No cross-talking or advice-giving. Don't give them advice at the end of the group, either. If someone asks for advice or assistance, then it is okay to speak your own truth in your turn. Otherwise keep quiet. Refrain from flip comments and making humorous additions to someone's story.

Listen from your heart, without judgment.

Look at the person speaking and give them your total attention. We have all been hurt by being ignored when we speak. Council circles can heal much of those wounds when each person pays deep attention to whoever is speaking.

What is spoken in circle remains in circle. This is a very important way to honor the sacred, healing, and ceremonial aspects of council. Confidentiality is a sacred covenant we make with one another. Don't refer to someone's story and don't bring up their story during a break or after the circle.

Appropriate release of anger is encouraged, but inappropriate raging is not. If there is a group member who uses rage inappropriately, warn the member about the behavior. If raging continues, you may have to ask them to leave the group. This also applies to individuals who "gender-bash."

Don't give unsolicited psychic readings or healings in circle. This is invasive of other people's boundaries and privacy. We are all intuitive and healers on some level, but we are in circle to do our own work.

Giving appreciation's to others after a deep sharing is a heartfelt and deep healing. Please do not refer to the person's material when doing so. The power of the appreciation's cannot be overstated. We begin to understand the positive effect we have on others in such a way that we can develop our spiritual identity and see where we fit into the larger Circle. In giving and receiving heartfelt appreciation's, we begin to see our gifts, our purpose in life. It is also the place where we practice love, where we learn to articulate the truth of the heart, where we learn to speak the heart's language. And we learn to receive gentle, loving information from others.

Emotional Release Guidelines

Doing these shamanic journeys will bring up deep emotions. When the speaker drops into deep space tears will rise to the surface. At this time the room blooms with a spiritual quality of high witness. Everyone in the circle is looking at the person speaking with 100% attention. The circle does not offer comfort, touch, or overly sympathetic gestures. Allow the process to continue unstopped. If you are timing people so everyone gets a turn, the person who holds the talking stick can be told the time gently and allow them to wrap it up. When done the stick is passed with dignity to the next person.

Working in this respectful way while sharing our own and other people's suffering develops both a spiritual and emotional discipline and maturity. These simple agreements when complied with, weave the net of safety necessary for the great descent into our sacred wound. The Alchemy work is pinpointed to bring up the pain and hidden information, that as we process and go deeper into, will reveal to us the secret of our destiny and life purpose. These sacred council agreements are vital and critical keys to our soul's journey and that discovery--and our healing.

Men's and Women's Group Work

Who can Facilitate both Gender's?

Teaching a co-ed group or two separate groups has it's difficulties-who's qualified to facilitate both men and women? Of course a man could facilitate the men's group and a women the women's group-and bring the two groups together for half of the meetings.

For a single person to facilitate both groups they must be able to not take either side--this requires a two-spirit person. This is someone who has the spiritual gifts and life purpose to work with both genders. A two-spirit person will not take sides and can sit as a "fair witness" among men and women. To work with both genders one must be impervious to sexual energy and have strong ethical boundaries. In no way is that position of facilitator or leader to be used in any form of "power-over" scenario! See chapter Twelve for further information on third gender folk and Chapter Thirteen on women's and men's combined work.

The Work

When men and women do this kind of deep spiritual and personal work together they sink into a field of intimacy that allows them to see each other in the highest possible way. We are all lifted within a sacred space. People can look like Gods or Goddesses. So one of the agreements is that there is no dating among group members during the class cycle. In this way we honor our inner work. We have all been in workshops where someone is sleeping with somebody else, and that energy creates a large gaping hole within the group. The Alchemy work is geared toward spiritual rebirth, and we do not need anything that may take our focus off that goal.

The guidelines discussed in this chapter will provide a strong vessel of integrity and safety in which to dismember outworn patterns and rebuild new ones with the help of spiritual friends and allies. This foundational work will provide profound insights and revelations. I hope many people will be called to work in both men and women's groups collectively as this provides enormous capacity to heal the wound between genders. I also wish that the two-spirit people will remember why they are here, find their life purpose and vocations, and bring that sacred gift to the people.

Part Two: Chapter Six

Shamanism, Initiation and Journeywork

The following work is based on the shamanic journey, that uses a drum or rattle to "drive" the journey. Give it a try, it has given millions of people results for thousands of years. There is a drumming session online at www.MedicineWomenLodge.com that you can use for this work.

What's a Shaman?

Many people today are very interested in shamanism, but they know little about it. They don't know the definition, the history, the cultural context, or the requirements for becoming a shaman. "Shaman" is a Tungus (Siberian) term that means, "One who sees in the dark," or healer. "Shaman" means medicine person or psychopomp (someone who helps the dead cross over). To become a shaman one must be initiated—instructed in esoteric or hidden knowledge—by the spiritual world. A shaman can be a woman or a man who is given gifts of power, healing, and knowledge by the spirits to become a mediator between the spiritual worlds and the people.

The stories we may hear or read about regarding shamanic initiations come to us from foreign countries, remote islands, and Native Americans. We may think these customs and tribal rituals are so unlike our European-based culture that we just can't relate to them. We in the West have lost most of our rites-of-passage rituals, forgetting why we need them. In considering these foreign customs, noted mythologist Joseph Campbell writes in *The Hero with a Thousand Faces* that "it becomes apparent that the purpose and actual effect of these [rituals] was to conduct people across those difficult thresholds of transformation that demand a change in the patterns not only of conscious but also of unconscious life."

But spirits don't go away. If shamanism is found all over the world, then our European ancestors must have practiced it in some form. Where did our Western heritage go? What did it look like when our predecessors actively practiced it? And what would a shamanic initiation look like inside the Western world today, with our busy lives, high-pressure jobs, automobiles, weekend workshops, computers, and instant information? How would an initiation by the spiritual world look to us personally?

A Call to a Healing Life Path

If a shaman is defined as a healer, medicine person, or psychopomp, then within our Western culture we have dreamers, artists, witches, priests, priestesses, healers, medical intuitives, midwives, and herbalists, among others, who might fit such a description. Not all these people are shamans, however. To become a shaman one is called, usually unwillingly. To be a shaman one is trained diligently by the spirits in the dreamtime, by another shaman, or by teachings in a near-death experience.

All stories recount the journey of the hero or heroine—how they overcome great obstacles and challenges to claim their destiny. What is usually called the crisis in a story plot is also an initiation. After undergoing that experience, the protagonist is reborn. Those stories are based on reality, and each of us is the protagonist within our own life story. Our lives present us with many obstacles that serve to initiate us. Initiation can mean different things to different people. Some initiations call the individual to a shamanic healing path, but most do not. Most initiations are calls of spirit to the individual to realign her or his life and behaviors in accordance with a higher purpose.

A Life Crisis as Initiation

These crisis events, traumatic and terrifying as they may be, are also the time-honored signposts of the "wounded healer" initiation. Since our Western shamanic culture was lost, we do not have a well-known framework to help people understand what it is to be "called" to a shamanic path or a healing path. Initiation into shamanism in particular can occur through hereditary transmission, dreams, near-death experiences, or traditional training in the techniques, names, and functions of the spirits, according to Mircea Eliade in his definitive book, *Shamanism: Archaic Techniques of Ecstasy.*

Carl Jung, the noted psychologist, also underwent a series of episodes during 1913–1917 that were shamanic in content. When Jung was assailed by dreams, voices, and visions, he had a choice: to fight them off or to voluntarily drop into the chaos. This experience shattered his life, but later it gave him his destiny, his calling, his right life path—archetypal depth psychology. Jung says of this experience in *Memories, Dreams, Reflections*; "...from the beginning there was no doubt in my mind that I must find the meaning of what I was experiencing in these fantasies. When I endured these assaults of the unconscious I had an unswerving conviction that I was obeying a higher will, and that feeling continued to uphold me until I had mastered the task." (p. 177)

During this stormy rite of passage, Jung came close to suicide. Some members of his profession think that Jung's descent was not so "voluntary" and could be defined as psychosis. Jung states his case like this, " It is of course ironical that I, a psychiatrist, should at almost every step of my experiment have run into the same psychic material which is the stuff of psychosis and is found in the insane. This is the fund of unconscious images which fatally confuse the mental patient. But it is also the matrix of a mythopoetic imagination which has vanished from our rational age.... Unpopular, ambiguous, and dangerous, [such an imagination] is a voyage of discovery to the other pole of the world." (Memories, Dreams, Reflections, pp. 188–189)

What happened to Jung is clearly a classic initiation experience when viewed through Western or shamanic lenses, and one of the gifts he developed as a result of that experience can be termed shamanic: his life-long study of dreamwork. His attention and respect for dreams developed through his European psychological framework, have their roots in many sacred spiritual traditions. Jung successfully went through his traumatic and dangerous passage, and in doing so he gained an empathetic understanding of suffering within the human psyche. This understanding enabled him to become a good healer, as only one who has suffered with the same illness can truly heal it. This is the wounded-healer initiation into a life path of service.

•The Shamanic Realms: the Three Sacred

•Worlds•

Many spiritual systems have divided the universe into three sections or levels. The upper level is called the upper worlds, the middle world is our Earth and present reality but it's spiritual counterpart, and the lower level is called the lower worlds. Both the upper and lower worlds are outside of time and are purely spiritual in nature. Each has different levels within it. Many religions and indigenous cultures have depicted these worlds using the Tree of Life. The Tree's mighty roots travel down to the lower worlds, the trunk fills our middle-world reality, and the arching branches and leaves take one into the upper worlds.

•The Upper World•

In the upper world we typically find beings in human form. The Elohim, the masters, teachers, shining ones, saints, Goddesses and Gods, our dearly departed family members, the ancestors, the ascended ones, Christ, Buddha, etc. To journey to the upper worlds, of course you will need to go up. You can travel on the branches of a tree, smoke, clouds, a ladder, or perhaps a bird will take you up, or you can fly up yourself. To reach the upper worlds and not just the top of the middle earth you will go through a threshold—a membrane, a door, a gate, an opening, or a landscape change. Then you will know you have reached the first level of the upper worlds.

•The Middle World•

Middle-world work is here on Earth, but in a spiritual counterpart. It is here we do astral projection, journey to gather information, travel across vast distances, and do diagnostic work with clients. The middle world is also where we find much negativity, including spirits of the dead who did not leave the Earth plane for various reasons. To start your journeywork it would be advantageous to limit your practice to the upper and lower worlds, which are filled with helping spirits.

•*The Lower World*•

The lower world is where you will find the power animals and totemic spirits. The lower worlds are also outside of normal time, and a journey there may feel like five minutes or half a lifetime. There are many realms to the lower worlds. To journey to the lower worlds you will need to drop into a tunnel through a hole, a river, an ocean, a cave, a tree, or as rain.

Shamanic Journeywork

Many times shamanic practitioners do not go into a lot of description or definition of the worlds because this can cause the participant to doubt their own experience—"Oh, she or he said that and then I experienced it, so maybe I just made it up based on what they said." Remember that these worlds are vast and fluid. Your spirits will work within your myths, books read, television shows watched, past history, secret desires, and your unconscious. If you find yourself in down in Alice's rabbit hole, which is a lower-world journey, or climbing a beanstalk to the upper world like Jack did, go for it. I always ask my students or clients to leave doubt by the front door, so when you are in your journey you are fully present. If you want, you can always pick up your doubt as you walk out to psychoanalyze your shamanic work. Practice. As you progress on your path using your different tools of discipline, accruing more and more experiences, you will eventually leave doubt in the dumpster because your life will be transformed and you will know.

Sensing in Journeys

Some people when they journey will have a pleasant reminder of childhood. We all journeyed as children into the hidden realms. Usually this memory leaves us at age eight or nine. But journeywork is easy. Some people see a movie screen suspended in front of their closed eyes, but most people don't. People tend to see light and dark, or colors, or pictures that come and go along with spirits talking to them. Or perhaps they just feel they know what is happening, or they taste or touch something in the journey. Validate all of your senses.

Here's a beginning visualization I give to nervous first-timers who have some performance anxiety. Close your eyes and imagine a lemon suspended in front of you. See the deep, rich yellow, smell the tartness, see the ridges and dimples as the lemon hovers in front of you. Now reach out and grab it out of the air. Immediately feel the weight of the lemon. Throw it up and down a few times. Now imagine you are just about to bite into it, through the skin and all. Your mouth may start salivating. Now in your imagination bite into the lemon. YOW! Feel the pucker and tartness hit the walls of your mouth and tongue. Now open your eyes. Good! That was your first creative visualization.

Visualization is a tool used by initiates in many traditions, especially so in the Western way. Jungians may call journeywork "creative imaging," which means traveling through our inner landscape or our psyche. Spiritual reality is both an inner and outer experience. The macro cosmos is in the microcosm.

At the very beginning of learning journeywork, "Just pretend." You are going to creatively visualize a hole in the ground, imagine jumping in, and then before you know it, the journey will have hooked you and you'll be off, experiencing it. Remember, leave doubt at the front door. If you ever find yourself in the journey losing focus, simply repeat your intention and your intention will bring you back.

To journey, you will need a drumming tape. You can make it yourself or buy one from a local store. The drumming tape is 30 minutes and if you are doing a 15 min journey, simple fast forward the tape to the middle. At the end of the drumming tape is a short call-back. This is when the fast continuous drumming stops with four counts of seven and then goes very fast. This is the call back. This means it is time for you to say good-bye, go back the way you came either up or down and return to your departure place. Always, always use the entire call-back time to reenter your body. This helps you complete the discipline of all shamanic practices-starting and ending sacred space. Many people prefer to journey in a darkened room or with a towel, handkerchief, or scarf folded over their eyes.

These basic journeys should be taken over and over to strengthen your discipline, focus your intention, and get you used to going into and out of the spiritual realms. Journeywork can be used in conjunction with dreaming practices. Diving into this deeper transpersonal arena will bring up emotions, repressed material, and shadow reflections, so make sure you have created a solid container of personal character to hold your experiences, both dream information and journeywork.

An important point to remember is that at any time in the journey you may stop what you are doing and come back. If you are not ready for a particular event that is presented to you, you may refuse it at that time. You have the ability to stop and end your journey if you need to.

Power Animals and Teachers

Totemic animal spirits are vast beings of enormous power. They are not just the representation of the animal here on Earth; they are also the guiding divine intelligence's that direct the spirit being. As we apply ourselves to our own awakening—raising shadow patterns to awareness, recognizing internal sabotage behaviors, using our dreams and journeywork skills, choosing creative change—over time our relationship with our power animals will develop into a strong, profound, numinous connection that surpasses words to describe. The animals can help us with any questions or topics, including emotional pain, trauma, decisions, career, sexuality, and health.

Totemic spirits and teachers may speak with you either literally or metaphorically. The spirits can use words or telepathy. They may also use a metaphorical language with you. The soul understands archetypes, symbols, and metaphors easily, and the dreamtime is composed of this story form of words.

The thing we must always remember about spirits is that they are not human. They are not attached to our lives in exactly the same way that we are. We are immersed in the physical world and see things through this narrow viewfinder. Spirits see the big picture and know more information: unconscious, conscious, past, present, and future. They are not limited to our mode of seeing.

When I say that the spirits bring gifts, I don't mean that once you journey and connect with your power animals you will have no worries, financial or otherwise. The spiritual world is not that interested in houses, money, and automobiles, although they recognize that we are very concerned with these topics. The spirits' primary goal is reconnecting us to our spiritual heritage and purpose, which is entirely different than what we may have in mind at times. Remember the old saying, "You will get what you need, not necessarily what you want." When I am working with animal spirits and teachers in my personal life, I do everything I can in the world using all available resources, creativity, and action to accomplish my goal. Then if things are not moving in a certain direction, I journey to the animals, ask questions and ask for a ritual to get the flow moving again.

This book is focused on giving you information and tools of self-empowerment. The idea isn't to do shamanic work or dreamwork so the spiritual world will just take care of us. Quite the contrary. As we come out of our own denial and heal ourselves, we are asked to take on more responsibility for our selves, our communities, and the Earth.

Ethics: Are You a Good Witch or a Bad Witch?

When journeying or working with ritual magic or asking for information in dreams, you must ask only questions concerning yourself, as it is not ethical to ask questions about someone else's life without their permission. For instance, you may want to know about a possible lover named Joey. Ethically, you cannot ask, "How can I make

Joey fall in love with me?" That is manipulation and is not ethical and will backfire on you. And I do not advise that you journey to "Joey's" spirit to request permission. Ask Joey directly and get permission, or do not do the journey on Joey. But you may ask, "What will Joey be like in relationship as a lover?" or "What is the lesson I will learn with Joey?" The spirits will show you many things in answer to these questions, and you can then make up your own mind about dating Joey.

A warning before you begin your shamanic work; your intention, whether for good or ill, will draw those experiences toward you. If you try to "force" the spiritual world to give you what you want, you are immediately heading toward black magic. Black magic is ego-oriented and intended toward personal power, manipulation, and control of the universe and others. The spirits may throw you some nasty curve balls to warn you off this path. On the other hand, if your intention is sincere the spirits will do all they can to help you as you aim toward health, healing, and personal transformation in an authentic and ethical manner.

How do you know when you are receiving accurate information? One way is that the teachers will speak with you in ways that lead you to greater understanding, deeper perspectives, show you your hidden agendas, and will emanate love or a strong authority. You will sense and feel their power, and the wisdom within the teachings. The teacher's counsel with love, wisdom and sometimes with a harsh voice of strength, if you need that in order to wake-up.

Lower World Journey to Meet Your Power Animals -15 Minutes

Visualize an opening into the Earth that you remember from some time in your life. Any entry into the ground—a cave, a spring, a tree stump, a hole made by a burrowing animal. The right opening will be the one that comes to you and feels right. If you dive into water, see a hole open where you will dive in. See your hole, remember your intention, and jump in to begin the journey. Go down through the opening and enter the tunnel. The tunnel may be dark or dim. If you run into any barrier go around it, or go through a crack. Don't try too hard. If you do this work correctly your journey will be relatively effortless.

You will emerge from the tunnel outdoors. Examine the landscape. You are looking for a power animal. Welcome the animal or animals that come to you. If no animal comes or awaits you, travel through the landscape, remembering its features. If you still encounter no animals, find another hole and jump down. Continue doing this until you establish contact with your animal friends.

When you find the animal, or it finds you, get to know it. Watch what it does. Typically animals start teaching us immediately. Then ask the animal how it will it work with you. What particular area of life is it going to help you with? How can you work with it, contact it, play with it, and what gift can you give it in return? If the animal wants you to travel with it, go! Explore, be active, ask questions. As the drumming begins to call you back to the middle world, thank the animal, and return up your tunnel and out of the hole, fully back into your body. Write down your journey in full detail.

Upper World Journey to Find Your Teacher-15 Minutes

To reach the upper world, you must pass through a threshold between it and the middle world. You will feel the difference. Start from your chosen place, and intend to go up. You can go up by using a tree, a ladder, a rope, flight, clouds, an arrow, smoke. View the landscape after you've entered the upper worlds. Remember your intention—you are looking for a teacher. Welcome the teacher that comes to you. If no teacher shows up, explore and look for one. If you cannot find one, find another way to go up to another level.

When you find the teacher, watch what is does. Listen for how it may speak with you, metaphorically or literally. The teacher will let you know what she or he wants from you. At the drumming call back, thank the teacher and dive down, through the threshold, and return fully into your body. Write down your journey in full detail.

Journey to find a Dream Helper-15 Minutes

A dream helper will teach you about your dreams; the obvious, the hidden, the forgotten aspects of your dream. A dream teacher may come from the upper or lower world. I would suggest when journeying to find a dream teacher to go to the spot of your departure place, state your intention and see who comes for you. If your lower world animal or teacher comes to take you to the lower world to introduce you to your dream teacher, then your dream teacher will be found in the lower world. If on the other hand, your upper world teacher comes for you, to take you up into the upper worlds to introduce you to your dream teacher, then, your dream teacher resides in the upper world. After this initial exercise when journeying to a dream teacher, you will know where you are going to find and speak to your dream teacher.

When you meet your dream helper introduce yourself, see where they live and ask how they will work with you. Ask for their help. Ask if they require anything from you. Write down your journey in full detail.

You may find your animal spirit or upper world teacher coming for you, or you may receive new teachers to help with your specific request in that certain area. This will give you a group of helpers and teachers who will give you plenty of information, inspiration, knowledge and direction.

Teachers

Journey's-go to your departure place, state your intention, example; My intention is to meet a teacher of Life-Purpose, or My intention is to meet a teacher of Relationships.

Journey to find a Teacher to help me with my Life-Purpose-15 Minutes

Journey to find a Teacher to help me with my Relationships-15 Minutes

Journey to find a Teacher to help me with my Sexuality-15 Minutes

Journey to find a Teacher to help with my Creativity-15 Minutes

You can take these basic journeys again and again. As you journey and map your lower and upper world regions, you will gather information that will be beneficial for your life. I suggest you do them many times in order to become proficient in contacting your helping spirits and teachers.

Chapter Seven
Soul Essence: Who Am I?

I have outlined journeys you can do to access information about internal patterns adopted in your family of origin, patterns you overlay in intimate relationships and in your sexuality, creativity, or right life path. I encourage you to ask your own questions of your teachers.

Exploring the Basic Construction of Your World View

In simplistic terms, our family, friends, and lovers make up a world view correlating to our beliefs and thoughts. We model our characters based on what we learn about gender roles and politics, social skills, and repressed shadow attributes from our families of origin, cultures, and communities. Much of the time we find we don't have cohesive ideas about who we are. Many of us tend to go from one thing to another without a great deal of inner reflection. The exercises presented in this chapter are designed to engage the mind and the dreaming body, and to draw up to consciousness an awareness of how we got to where we are.

People tend toward two distinct personality types—clingers or distancers. We usually know immediately which one we are, whether we generally hang on to people or push them away. If we are clingers we may draw distancers into our intimate lives. If we are distancers we may get into relationship with clingers. We draw our opposite or our twin personified into relationship in order to heal the wound of "not enough" or "too much." This is useful self-knowledge for reflection.

Family Systems and Gender Roles

In your journal write, "Mother, Sisters, Female Friends, Women." On another page write, "Father, Brothers, Male Friends, Men." List the positive and negative attributes of the female principles as you've experienced them in your life, then do the same for the masculine principles. Note the positive qualities and attributes of both the men and women. This was also something you learned. Since we are concentrating on discovering limiting patterns we are focusing on negative contracts. In relation to your mother and father, ask yourself the following questions. The answers will give you a good idea of which patterns, role models, and gender norms you watched and perhaps adopted as your own.

How did your father treat your mother? In a patriarchal manner, like a slave, contemptuously? Or did he love her, laugh a lot, dance with her? Was he faithful or unfaithful to her? Did they stay married or get divorced? Was he a powerful man? Did he give his power to women?

How did your mother treat your father? Did she wait on him hand and foot? Did she resent him? Did she love him and honor him? Did she have affairs? Was she a powerful women? Did she give her power to men? Did she have her own life, creative or otherwise?

By their actions, what did your parents teach you about men?

By their actions, what did your parents teach you about women?

Did they abuse each other? Did they abuse you? How? What effect has this had on you? In what areas?

If you are male, do you find you treat women like your father did? Or completely the opposite?

If you are female, do you find you treat men like your mother did? Or completely the opposite?

How do you treat people of your same gender? Do you have deep and abiding friendships?

This exercise, as simple as it is, can be very difficult for people—some go blank and just cannot remember. So in class we work with it in a group format with the entire circle helping. To help you access the information without a group, you can journey on any of these questions. I recommend that you do one journey on each question for 15–20 minutes. In your dream journal, write down in detail what you received: impressions, feelings, metaphors, information.

Personal Power & Negative Contracts

The phrases "negative contracts" and "negative agreements," are apt ways to codify our shadow interactions with others. Negative agreements are dysfunctional energy dynamics between two people or within a group of people. In many of our relationships we are in "power-over" or "power-under" scenarios. These are negative agreements that may have kept us safe and seemingly in control of our life, but they also limit us while showing a false persona to the world. We did choose this mode of being in the past, and we sometimes forget that we can make new choices and redirect our energies.

To reclaim personal power means coming out of denial and choosing positive action and creative directions for ourselves. To move into our power means taking a fair and critical look at our lives to see where fear is blocking us from making changes and, therefore, growing.

Where There is Fear, There is Power Denied

Where there is fear, there is power denied. Denial simply means saying no to life in some form or another. Saying no is usually a cover for fear of failure, fear of success, fear of change, fear of power, fear of responsibility, fear of authenticity, fear of intimacy, fear of getting bigger, fear of being killed, fear of service, fear of misuse of power, fear of not being loved, fear of loving yourself enough to be whole. The list is endless. We need to recognize and identify our fears, then decide whether we want to end our negative agreements.

How to Recognize a Negative Agreement

So how do you recognize negative contracts? Simple. What is making you miserable? What in your life is causing restlessness, frustration, anger, resentment, depression, fear, anxiety, denial, or addiction? Whatever relationship these emotions are spinning around, there you will find a negative contract simmering to the boiling point. Ask yourself these questions:

Who do I feel is limiting me? Squelching me? In what ways? Why?
Who do I think is lying to me? Why?
For whom am I making excuses or covering up? Why?
About *what* am I always complaining? Why?
About *whom* am I always complaining? Why?

Whomever you are constantly thinking about, compulsively or obsessively, there resides a negative contract. Sounds like shadow material, doesn't it? Yes, negative contracts can be laced with shadows and that can make them harder to identify, since we're often projecting our unconscious material onto others. If we are compulsively talking about somebody else (because "it's so obviously about them"), then we may be in the grip of our shadow. The stuff we are projecting onto the other person is really our stuff. This shadow material may help us identify where we are manipulating or hurting others. Samples of covert negative agreements include:

Whoever brings home the most money tends to have the power in a couple. This is a tough agreement to break, as it tends to be a covert one. The one who is financially dependent may be afraid the financial support will be withdrawn if they make waves.

A teacher may disempower her or his students by accepting their bright shadow projections. The students' part of the contract is their willingness to give their power to the teacher.

An employer, co-worker, or friend may mistreat us, and we put up with it because we are afraid of being fired, talked about, disliked, or alone.

Once we start recognizing our negative contracts we may get angry at the other person or group. Remember, this is always a two-way street. We are getting something out of the agreement as well. What is it? Explore your reality deeply. We do not necessarily need to leave the person or group with whom we have negative contracts. If we want to reclaim authentic personal power, we *do* have to stop silently colluding with them. We can discuss our ideas about the relationship and the power dynamics and suggest a healthier way of relating. If the other person or group does not agree with you or denies the out-of-balance dynamic, you will have to decide whether you are willing to leave.

Journeywork on Negative Contracts

Students always ask me whom they should seek out in journeys, their power animal or their teacher? In my journeys, I simply ask the question and whoever comes for me is the one I follow. Here are some journey questions about negative contracts. I encourage you to ask questions pertinent to your life. *Again, I recommend one question per journey.* This is because each individual journey will deepen your connection and build on the last one. Each journey can be 15 minutes in length.

What negative contracts am I in with my father? How does my father take my power? Why do I allow it? How do I take my father's power, and why does he allow it?
What lessons am I learning through my negative contracts with my father?
How can I heal the negative agreements with my father?
What negative contracts am I in with my mother? How does my mother take my power? Why do I allow it? How do I take my mother's power, and why does she allow it?
What lessons am I learning through my negative contracts with my mother?
How can I heal the negative agreements with my mother?
How did I internalize my parents' gender roles? How did I buy into their beliefs and behaviors about men and women?
What negative contracts am I in with the men in my life? How do my male lover, friends, and employers take my power and why do I allow it? How do I take men's power and why do they allow it?
What am I learning from my negative contracts with men? How can I heal those contracts?

What negative contracts am I in with the women in my life? How do my female lover, friends, and employers take my power and why do I allow it? How do I take women's power and why do they allow it?

What am I learning from my negative contracts with women? How can I heal these contracts?

You may have other journey questions you'd like to ask. Remember, this is not about making your parents—or your lover or employer or friend—wrong or blaming them. They did not "do it" to you. Relationship is a two-way street, and you are there, too. These exercises are to give you an idea of how you chose certain beliefs or behaviors, so you can now take a mature look at whether and why you want to continue to choose them and keep acting on your worldview.

Making Choices about Contracts

As you see the consequences, good and bad, of your beliefs and behaviors, you have to decide whether you want to continue a particular pattern. Many readers will ask, "Why on earth would I choose to continue a pattern where I get hurt or give myself away?" My reply: One, we are interacting in relationships that have some meaning for us. Two, we are receiving something out of those behaviors and patterns. Three, we many not awaken to all our negative agreements at once. And four, it is not quite so simple.

Reading about negative contracts and identifying them is one thing, but changing them is another.

Because negative contracts are based on long-term patterns of relating and can be attached to childhood trauma, it may take us considerable and concerted effort to disengage from a negative behavior, relationship, or group and create new patterns. As negative contracts involve other people or groups, they have to be addressed with those other people. How will you do that? Will you evade the issue by leaving? Or will you address the problem, as you see it, directly? The other people will have their say, too. You may be surprised at what they say back to you. This is a risk, as you may not like what you hear, but this begins the dialogue. Perhaps they will hear you. However, be warned that people who are engaged in negative contracts do so (as you do) for a reason. If it still serves them, even if the consequences are hurting them or you, they may not hear you at all when you talk about ending the contract. You may be spitting in the wind for all they care. If they refuse to acknowledge what you are saying, and even go so far as to tell you that you're crazy, what then?

Authentic Listening

Some people will hear what you are saying, they may also have felt something uncomfortable between the two or you or within the group context. This is a good sign. If folks are willing to listen with their hearts, the limiting patterns of communication can be dissolved with mutual goodwill for all. Conflict when addressed by willing parties will strengthen the relationships. Speak about what goes on, how you feel and what you want, and outline ways that the relationship may work or flow better.

But be forewarned. When you confront someone by speaking out in a conscientiousness manner and giving voice to the lie, what do you suppose may be their response? "Oh, you're right! I am so sorry! Let's start all over!" Not usually. People tend to defend their behaviors, sometimes aggressively. This is why it may not be as easy as it seems to end a negative contract. Negative agreements are built on fears, silence, collusion, and secrecy. They are limiting and binding. If the other person involved says, "It is not so," "I'm not doing that," "Well, dear, that is your experience, not mine," or any of the hundreds of other refuting responses, you are left with a choice. Here's the hard part. You must ask yourself, "Am I willing to stand up for what I believe to be authentic and ethical?" If you are, this may leave you with a still harder choice: "Am I willing to be alone rather than continue in patterns of behavior that are not healthy for me?"

Supporting Your Authentic Self

This is the real test. It doesn't so much matter whether you are right in your position. It matters that you are being hurt or are colluding with hurting someone else. It matters that you speak up and give voice to the lie. This gets it out of your body. If you are unwilling to speak up, that is OK. You may choose to leave without talking about the negative contract. There will be other occasions for direct communication, as this is a life lesson we all have to learn, and you will encounter it again and again. It matters what action you take when confronted with denial. What will you do?

Many people at this point start to rationalize so they can stay within the context of the relationship or group. Whether it is your job, your boyfriend or girlfriend, or a group of some sort, you can pull out all kinds of reasons why you have to endure it. This is OK, too. But there is a problem within this that you will soon discover: you are aware of what is going on underneath the outer form of the relationship. And you don't like it. This will cause you frustration, anger, and resentment, and, like a burr under a saddle, sooner or later this will make you kick at the traces. You will probably do many mental re-runs of why they should change or why you should leave, until you either explode or implode with holding your self-deception, or change will become more preferable to this endured hell. You will prefer to be alone than to put up with this kind of pain any longer. You will create the change and move on.

That is personal power. It is harder than it looks. You may find yourself leaving—or at least radically changing—one or many forms of relationships as you come to grips with who you are. This includes friends, lovers, perhaps a husband or wife, and jobs. In this process you are forming the foundation stone of your spiritual intent for inhabiting a human body and how you will move through the world. These are your character qualities put into action. This is activating your spiritual intent and calling in your self-authenticity and personal power.

It may be painful instigating the necessary leave-taking, but afterwards, the good news is, when we dissolve our negative agreements we free up a tremendous amount of creative energy. It can feel like we are reborn of spirit. We can feel exactly like a caterpillar emerging on a warm spring day as a butterfly. We feel full of life and want to spread our wings and fly. It is as if we are waking up from a foggy sleep. This energy can be used to create empowered relationships and new, healthier ways of relating.

The old saying, "Birds of a feather flock together," is an accurate wisdom expression. You will find that you will draw a different energy of people to you as you express more of your personal power. They will match your own hard-won ground of being, and your freedom and range of expression with these people will elevate you to new heights. You will begin to see and identify negative contracts within a shorter time and will implement changes with less and less fuss, less and less blame. You will simply make the changes needed inside the relationship or move on to greener pastures.

Learning and Integrating the Lessons

After doing the above work, you will have a much larger context for your personal story. Some may feel chagrin at seeing who is pulling their strings or at discovering that they are pulling other people's strings. If you are upset at seeing your covert negative agreements, I congratulate you. It takes guts, willingness, and courage to see and identify where we are participating in perpetuating negative contracts. You may feel some shame or disgust at yourself or others. It is OK to feel that as it shows your conscience is intact and talking with you. You may even find yourself steaming and angry at what you discover, either about yourself or others.

Used in positive ways this anger can give you the power, the force you require to move forward. It is better not to steamroller folks with your "aha" realizations, though. It is better to use that energy to sit with your insights and meditate on them, talk them over with dear friends, and do more shamanic journeys to learn how to get out of the negative contracts in a healthy manner. Eventually we will forgive ourselves and others as we see how each negative agreement provided a valuable lesson in recognizing personal patterns and self-authenticity.

Personal Mission Statement: To Be or Not to Be

Usually, after discovering how we lost ourselves or were misdirected in a negative contract, we say things like, "I will never do that again! How could I? I will see that coming next time!" A good way to use this energy is to direct it into forming a mission statement outlining your personal code of ethics. This is a manifesto of personal authenticity and positive agreements. When the statements are completed, you can go into ritual space and take your vows to yourself and the listening spiritual beings. This is a decisive act of personal power: taking responsibility for your thoughts and actions regarding your personal relationships, your do's and don'ts. Print your statement of personal purpose on beautiful paper, frame it, and hang it on your wall as a reminder of your agreements between you and the ancestors.

Where is Your Life Leading You?

We all engage in some forms of negative agreements with people. Over the course of our lives this is where many of our most powerful lessons originate. By taking stock of where we are now, from where we came we can access how far we have traveled.

Our life paths are individual, and we each use many different tools for our transformation. Where is your life leading you? Where are you now? What have you discovered by walking your path? Where have you seen or felt the grace of spirits in your life? Start in the beginning at the time of your childhood and continue into adulthood and the present. Take some time and write about your journey. I suggest twenty pages. In the writing you will have to think backward from who you are now to who you were then.

The benefits of this exercise are tremendous and cannot be overstated. Your writing will give you a mythic outline of your heroic journey. By starting at the beginning, you go back to your beginner's mind, which will bring back to you your young self—the one who had hopes, dreams of greatness, faith, and expectancy. As you go forward, you will see the obstacles and challenges that beset you, and how you handled them (or tried to avoid them). You'll see what hopes and dreams you gave up, deleted, or changed, and when. You'll learn how these challenges contributed to the negative contracts you now find yourself in.

Feel free to journey on why those obstacles or challenges were given to you. Doing this work in a group or with your therapist is a good idea, as you may discover much with the help of your spiritual teachers that you did not know. In your review, you will begin to see the fine hands of spirit in the twists and turns of your personal life. Take some time to think about how your sacred wound deepened you. How did those experiences crack you open to spirit? How did spirit enter you? Help you? What are the gifts of your wound? What could you do with these gifts? How could you incorporate what you are learning or have learned into your life or livelihood? How can you share what you learned with others? In the end, you will have a better idea of *why* you are who you are today.

Chapter Eight

Life Purpose: Why Am I Here?

Career vs. Destiny

All my life I have loved talking with people and listening to them tell their stories. Elders especially I would ask, "What happened to you? What has your life been like? How did you get through?" They would look at me, delighted that they had a willing ear, and launch in—regaling me with stories of courage, adventure, and great-heartedness. I never get tired of listening to them drop into the mystery of their lives. It is like tracking spirit.

For instance, it amazed me to hear how a farm boy in Ohio just up and left one day, hitched a ride to the sea, and worked on ships as he traveled all over the world. His life events led him to meet a man who mentored him. He ended up studying engineering in Italy, and he became the top international recognized engineer. I loved hearing how he fought for fair wages and won, despite enormous resistance. I wondered what prompted him to leave the farmhouse that day? What led him to that boat where he met the mentor for his life work? What voice called to him?

A woman I'll call Shannon described her father as an angel. I said, "Tell me about him." She told me a wonderful true tale set in the 1950s. Her mother, Meg, had been married twice to very abusive men. She had a child with each husband. She divorced each of the men and eventually became a single mother with two children to raise. When she met Jim, she knew he was different. They fell in love and married, and he adopted the two children as his own. When she was eight months pregnant with Shannon, her abdomen swelled gigantically with their baby. Jim and Meg would meet at bars, pretending to be strangers. She would order, "A drink for that gentlemen down the bar." He would thank her and ask her to dance, which they did with her distended belly pushing up between them. They loved each other.

Meg was in her teens when she first married and had children. She did not know how to raise a child, keep house, or cook. Jim taught her how to speak to children, what to do, what not to do. He taught her how to cook and dress, balance a check register, keep account of her own money, and tend the house well for her children. He took her under his wing and taught her the basic social skills she'd never had the chance to learn. He adored her and she adored him. It was a match made in heaven.

Jim served as an officer in the air force. Lately, he had taken on the military when he discovered faulty mechanisms in the aircraft that would lead to plane crashes if not corrected. He was raising hell because the men were in danger. He was making trouble for himself, but he continued. One night, Meg dreamt that he died in a plane crash. She awoke sobbing, begging him not to go on any more flights. But how could he do that? He was in the air force. He told her not to worry, everything would be fine. Nevertheless, he made out a will, went through all the bills, and paper-clipped notes to each one. "In case anything ever happens to me," he said, "do this marked #1 first, this marked #2 second, and so on." He led her through it step by step.

A few months later Jim went up in a chopper with four men; he was assigned to the right-hand position riding shotgun. With them was a sergeant, Otto, who disliked Jim intensely and tried every chance he got to needle, provoke, and bully him. Jim did not let Otto bother him. The sergeant was sitting behind the pilot. The helicopter took off, hovering about ten feet above the ground. Just before its final sweep upward, Jim yelled, "Hey! Stop the chopper, set it down!" The pilot landed the craft. Jim said he wanted to change seats with Otto, so they did, and then the helicopter took off again. Sometime during that flight, the faulty machinery failed and the chopper crashed. The only person killed was the one sitting directly behind the pilot—Jim.

This is a true story. My heart exploded with love and my eyes filled with tears as Shannon shared it with me. That is a mystery play. Jim came into Meg's life, loved her, and taught her to be a woman and mother. He was fighting with the air force to replace the faulty machinery because men were being placed in danger. After hearing Meg's premonition dream, Jim could have tried to avoid what the dream foretold. He knew (unconsciously) what was going to happen, and he spent time arranging the family's affairs and instructing Meg in how to care for them. Then he switched seats with the sergeant, a man who had been out to get him. That was an act of love.

It is my belief that Jim's soul was presented with a choice: he could stay in his seat and live, continue to be with his wife and children, or save the life of an enemy and die for a cause he believed in—the safety of his men. He could have avoided death, but he chose not to. Do you think Sergeant Otto got it? That Jim gave his life for him? What did Otto do with that? How did that change him? Jim *was* an angel. That is a life of Christ consciousness in action. We usually don't know what is going to happen in our lives. The human heart has tremendous courage, and many times this courage is activated when we help others. While we can't say whether Jim made the right or wrong decision in that helicopter, we can know that he made a decision based on love.

Hey! That's Not My Destiny!

What do we do when our destiny shows up and it's not what we expected or hoped for? Jim may have thought he would live to a ripe old age and play with grandchildren. He wanted, I am sure, many more lazy summer days to make love with his wife, eat dinners on picnic benches spread with red-and-white-checkered cloths, drink beer, and say good night to his three children. Instead, he chose a mystery play. He gave a gift of love and a helping hand wherever he went.

All of us are presented daily with life challenges in which we can choose responses based in love or fear. You have probably heard that before, read it before, and maybe quoted it to your best friend before. Yet do you know how many of us do not make a choice to free ourselves toward more creative actions? I have worked with many women who, for fear of taking financial responsibility for themselves, rationalize why they stay in their miserable marriages. Depressing marriages in which they are dying, desiccating, withering. They will try another workshop, take another class, do therapy, yet they are unwilling to make the choice that is looking them in the face; creative change, personal freedom, self-responsibility.

There are a lot of good workshops out there with many excellent teachers, but teachers cannot save you. They cannot make the leap over the chasm that is staring you in the face. Only you can do that. If you want, go ahead and fight it. Fight it with all you've got. Take that choice and try to beat it into submission. It won't go away.

We are all destined for greatness. Acknowledging that fact doesn't indicate pathological narcissism or a need for continual ego embellishment; it's simply the recognition that each and every one of us is a God or Goddess in miniature. We have the seeds of greatness in our hearts and souls. We all need healthy grandiosity. We all need encouragement.

The Choice: To Allow or Block Destiny

Not-knowing is the void. Chaos. Gestation of the unknown. We are caught between two worlds: the old, familiar, safe one and the new, untried, scary one. We are caught in a paradox, a situation that seems contradictory. Usually what we want to do is figure it out, categorize it, and fill the void with something. Immediately.

Sometimes in my classes students may get mad at me or another participant and use this as an excuse to leave. This way, they figure, their destiny will leave them alone, and they will not have to really change. I have news: making the teacher or another group member wrong will not make your purpose go away. You are being called. You know who you are. If you resist that call, the pressure will intensify, the inner turmoil will crank up, and your life may fall apart. You may even lose everything. Then you will listen, just as I finally did. So. What creative change is calling you? What is it you really want to do? What are the reasons that you cannot ever imagine doing this one incredible feat?

Just start toward it. Take one step at a time. Your life path is different; you are a singular individual with a destiny that is calling you. We think that if we take one baby step that's all we have to do. Come on. The world is filled with millions of opportunities for creativity and abundance. But first you might have to clear some room in your life for something new to enter. Yes, you are being asked to give something up: self-sabotage patterns, the nay-saying critical voice, the procrastinator, or the busy beaver that does for other people first, you last. This can take some time.

You may have to wait for destiny's timing. You may be ready before your destiny is. Or you may not think you are ready when you are. Destiny includes issues other than career. Destiny also includes your partner or beloved, your sexuality, your health, your creativity, your home, and your friends. Yes, you do have free choice. You can resist change. You can resist growth. But if you do, you will only become more miserable. Whether you allow or fight your destiny determines your mental, emotional, and physical health.

What is Knocking?

Something is knocking on your door, stalking your dreams. It approaches you when the lights are turned off. Something is on your mind. Listen to it. Give it an ear. It won't eat you—it simply wants you to listen to it before it's forced to create chaos in your life to get your attention. Resisting that voice will drain your energy. Many people have a stranglehold on their dreams, all the while complaining to their friends, therapist, teachers that they are miserable. They don't realize how much precious energy they are using, killing off their own dreams.

For some people all their resistance, nasty feelings, low self-esteem, and denial will come up during the back-and-forth process of, "Will I, won't I, will I, won't I, will I, won't I join the Dance?" This is when the real fighting takes place, in the psyche. When they finally take the leap and make a decision they go full steam ahead. Some people, on the other hand, make a decision, then perform very poorly and say, "See? I told you I couldn't do it!" Or they drop out of the program, class, university, writing, painting, jogging, whatever, and tell you, "It came to me that I'm not to do it after all, and I am so relieved! Really!" Who are they kidding? Me? It feels like they are throwing fuzz balls into the air to somehow fog my consciousness into agreeing with them.

They are trying to get consent in their negative contract with themselves.

Have you done this yourself? Or do you have a friend like that? It's best to let go of being their A-1 Supporter for Personal Change and allow them their patterns. They will do it in their own time, or they won't. You, meaning you and I, have plenty of work getting our own lives into alignment. It is easy to judge others who do not make the moves we think they should. That way we get to feel superior. Right? Best thing to do is to bless them and send them love. Do the same for yourself. We always have to remember timing. Forcing our timing onto other people is not fair to them and it creates friction. We may do this because we are unwilling to look at ourselves, or we may see how clearly they are hurting. So allow your destiny to come to you, and allow others their own timing.

Spiritual Gifts

Spirit gifts can define our spiritual path, our destiny, or our employment in a right life path. Don't know what gifts you have? One way to determine your spiritual gifts is to figure out how spirit talks with you. Writing a miniature autobiography is an excellent tool for accessing this information. Take five sheets of paper and write down, from childhood on, what significant, spiritual, or sacred events have happened to you. When you write your autobiography, think about your "fantasies" from childhood. What were they? Write them down. What were your grandiose dreams? What sacred experiences have you had that perhaps scared you? Write those down, too. This information is not just for defining gifts and life path; it is also essential information and validation that spirit has talked with you in some way during your life. This can point out how you can develop your spiritual path.

One woman, as a child, used to see fairies in the rays of the sun falling across her bed. She also was given messages from these tiny creatures. She would be flooded with feelings of joy and oneness during these experiences. One day she wanted to share the joy with her mother. When she tried, her mother denounced her experience and said she was making it up. From that day on, the girl would not allow herself to see the sun fairies. This caused her great sadness and isolation. As an adult, when she confronted the split between her mother and her psychic gifts, she was able to resolve the conflicting loyalty bind she felt, which brought on a reconnection to spirit.

A man when out in nature experiences an intense energy emanating from trees, rocks, and earth. In nature, he feels completely connected to himself and the world. The more time he spends in nature, the stronger his body awareness grows. He begins to have powerful dreams of earth spirits. Over time he is able to incorporate this energy to help overcome his fear of the spiritual worlds.

A woman shared that while lying in bed she occasionally experiences the energy of the Divine Feminine coming into her body!

We are so used to negating our inner spiritual experiences because we've learned to believe that sacred experiences aren't normal. Another great way to uncover your gifts is to find a friend or group with whom you can share your dreams, psychic gifts, and intuitions. With the help and intention of other people around you, make your gift as normal as seeing, hearing, touching. It is normal to talk to spirit in some way. What is abnormal is our society cutting us off from direct contact with spirit. Allow yourself that contact as you consider the following.

Life Purpose Questionnaire
What have you always longed to do? To be?
What stops you from doing it?

Make a list of all the reasons why doing this would be good for you and the healthy changes that would occur.

Make a list of all the reasons why doing this *seems* impossible to do.

Make a list of all your fears.

Make a list of action steps—activities that lead you in the direction of your desired goal (gathering information on class schedules, fees, materials needed, etc.)

Journey to Soul Essence -20 min

Another way to uncover information on your soul's gifts is to do a shamanic journey to obtain information regarding your soul and its natural gifts. Remember, if you don't know who to ask, whether to seek out your lower-world power animals or upper-world teachers, simply repeat your intention and see who comes for you.

For this journey, give yourself 20 minutes of drumming; make sure the tape has a call-back section at the end. You will be traveling out of your body and present life to view your soul essence before you incarnated. Remember, in journeywork you travel beyond the boundaries of ordinary time and space, and you can go forward or backward in time. When you arrive at that place before you were born, you can either see yourself as separate or you may merge with your soul essence. While viewing or merging with your soul essence, ask yourself these questions:

What colors am I?
What music or sound am I?
What texture am I?
Am I hot? Am I cool?
Am I fire, water, earth, or air?
What words would describe my essence?

When you hear the drumming call back, return fully to the middle world and your body. Spend some time with the answers and insights you received during your journey. Now take the time to draw a picture of your soul essence. You can use crayons, paints, oil-pastels, anything as long as it is color. Instead of drawing you can cut out pictures from magazines and form a collage. Create a portrait of your soul. It can be abstract or representational. It can be a mandala, geometric designs, or flowing watercolors. When you are done, keep it in your personal journal or use it as an altar piece.

Journey to a Teacher for Help with Life Purpose 20min

If you have not done a journey to find a teacher who will help you with your life purpose, this is a good time. Remember that the teacher who comes for you may be your power animal or upper-world teacher. Either one is fine. Go to your departure place and state your intention—"I am asking for a teacher to help with my life purpose." See who comes for you, and follow them. They may be a teacher from either the lower world or the upper world. Take at least 20 minutes for this journey. Ask specific questions, such as:

What am I here to do?

What are my spiritual gifts?

What is my life purpose? (This could be a doing or being quality.)

Is my life purpose also to be my career?

What specific lessons do I need to learn before manifesting this? What specific action steps do I need to take?

Don't Worry, Be Happy

Your life does not have to be perfect, with your lover just so, or your career skyrocketing, to allow yourself the pleasure and satisfaction of being alive. Life is good. Create your personal space as an altar to your life. Make your room a temple. Allow your soul to connect with the living reality of your home, family, friends, nature, and Source.

What in your life is working? What do you have to be grateful for? When was the last time you thanked the great spirit for your life? Your destiny may pick you up when you are fifty-three. It may grab you at six years old. You may be solving the riddle of your life even as you read this. You may be a gift to others simply by being who you are. Underneath, deep down, smack in the middle of your heart you are being called. What is that call saying to you? What are you waiting for? Come on in, the water's fine.

Chapter Nine

Relationships & Sexuality

We yearn for union. To be whole. To surrender to love. To be at peace. To feel bliss. To manifest our destiny. To gather together the scattered and lost parts of ourselves, separate out that which no longer serves us, and melt down the rest into a new metal. Alchemical gold, that which sustains light and is formed of light. Spiritual transformation, no small task.

We also long for connection. We want that special someone who will form the "other half" of our circle—our soulmate, our beloved. We may have a group of friends yet still feel alone in the world. Many people today, having no real sense of community, live in isolated units either as singles or couples.

Putting the Sacred Back in Sex

Many of the books are on Tantra, or sacred sexuality, which brings the spiritual back into the physical component of sexuality. By honoring both the Goddess and the God within each individual, we lift ourselves into the sacred space of Krishna and Rada, the divine lovers. This helps give us a focus on the union of sex completely different than our Western religious sin-and-sex scenario. Any work in this area will help heal the wound the church has given the human body.

Much of the information on sacred sexuality is needed as many of us did not grow up with sex education or parents who took the time to teach us about the trials and errors of first attempts, misguided hormones, and the leaps of deep intimacy. So it is very convenient to go to a local store and peruse the different books exploring sexuality. But they can offer only intellectual knowledge. Sex is the experience, after all, not talking about it or reading about it.

Relationships are more than Sex

Sustaining an intimate relationship requires more than great sex, even if the sexual connection is spiritual and ecstatic. Relationships also require well-honed communication skills, which depend on our awareness of self and other and an understanding of the qualities of different ways of speaking and listening. Can we express our thoughts and feelings clearly, without blame? Can we truly hear the other person when they speak? We need to understand our patterns—how we manipulate words to get what we want, how we fight. We must do some inner work on the shadow. And we must consider what kind of work our partner has done in the inner territory of their psyche.

Throw into that mix our likes and dislikes, our self-esteem or lack of it, how needy we are at any given time, our willingness to forgive and keep striving for intimacy, how quickly we leave when the going gets difficult.... All of this affects the intimate side of the relationship, our sex life. The success of our relationships boils down to whether we can inhabit our body consciously as we are in communion with another.

One of the primary components to an effective and ongoing love relationship is rarely if ever mentioned in lists of requirements: spiritual compatibility. By this I do not mean being of the same religious background or sharing a practice of a spiritual path, though that can help. I mean that spirit is the essential ingredient in all relating, and it's important to have a spiritual ground of being where you both can meet.

For much of my life I hid my spirituality from others, so I dated men who had no real spirituality. The superficiality of these dating encounters were extremely painful to me, yet I could not put my finger on why. For the most part they were *nice* guys. But the nice guys didn't do it for me. Without that spiritual juice between us I felt flat and unfulfilled.

Dating for the Soul

This problem comes from holding the tension of opposites. When we are being called to soul emergence, we can feel it first as a low-level frustration with our daily activities. This tension causes us to begin the process of expanding our soul outward; we don't know where we're going, but we are searching, restless. However, in our daily activities we try to pretend everything is hunky-dory. So we are holding two opposing realities or tensions within our soul. If we can hold this tension long enough until we leap forward to our true destiny, we will transition successfully from an old way of being to an new one.

If we are dating a nice guy or girl, we may keep trying to fit them into our old pattern of relating. We may desperately cling to them because we are afraid of the changes that we feel are coming but have not yet arrived. This is living in between, in limbo. It is living in a paradox, and that is uncomfortable. But the real issue isn't the other person; it's the current situation of soul expansion, the consequences of working with spiritual reality and developing the soul in connection with spirit. This changes us from the inside out. We are no longer able to accept a superficial form of communication and relationship.

If you have taken a look at your sub-strata psyche and deeply faced your shadow material, then you have been—or are being—alchemized, melted down, changed, transformed into something else. Gold. It does not behoove you to judge others as "less than" if they have not done this work. It behooves you to find a partner who is your spiritual match.

Someone you can talk to about your sacred experiences and your spirituality.

Some people who engage in spiritual work will be perfectly content in life partnerships with folks who could care less about spirituality. Good, as long as they both are truly involved and loving with each other. But for those of you who are dating, dating, dating and not finding someone who blows your bells and whistles, you might consider whether you are dating a soul who resonates with yours. It really doesn't matter what your partner looks like or how good sex is with them. If you are spiritually inclined and are dating a spiritual wasteland, if you are feeling frustrated and judging your partner harshly because of it, perhaps you are caught in a negative contract of your own devising.

Journey to Meet Your Soul 20min

Our ancient mystery traditions tell us that our soul's gender is the opposite of our physical gender. One of the ways to meet your soul, your counterpart, is to journey inward and meet the divine masculine or the divine feminine. This is the aspect we tend to project out onto our intimate others. This journey will introduce you to your other half, your ally, your beloved.

This 20 minute journey can be done many times, but for now begin a dialogue with your inner beloved. When you state your intention, you can journey inward. Here are some suggestions for individual journeys.

My intention is to meet my soul.
My intention is to ask my soul what he or she wants from me.
My intention is to ask my soul how I mistreat her or him, and how I do this to the men and women in my life.
My intention is to ask my soul how we can come into an inner alignment or sacred marriage.

When you hear the call back, remember to come completely out of your journey and fully inhabit your body. Write down what your soul told you, all the thoughts and feelings. Don't be surprised if your soul showed you various aspects of yourself that you may or may not have liked. This is all good work and marks the beginning of a long and fruitful relationship. The more you get to know your inner soul, the more cohesive and integrated you will become, with more to offer to others in your life.

Journey to a Teacher to Help with Relationship

Issues 15min

I suggest that you do this journey for 15 minutes the first time. As with all the journeys in this book, you can repeat it several times, perhaps for longer periods as you need more time. Relationship issues include aspects of your personal story, your family's stories, and much shadow material.

Go to your departure place and state your intention—that you'd like to meet a teacher to help you with relationships. You can ask your power animal or general teacher to introduce you. Follow whoever comes for you into the upper or lower worlds. The teachers know who you are, where you come from, your current life lessons, and your past. They will reveal valuable information to you during your journey. Remember to use the entire call back to come into your body. Write down what you learn in each journey.

Journey to a Teacher of Sacred Sexuality 15min

If you have not taken the time to journey for a teacher who will help you understand sexuality, you may do so now. If you encounter resistance to the teacher who shows up (as with any of these journeys), choosing to move through the resistance will gift you with a spiritual lesson.

To start—I suggest a 15-minute journey—begin from your point of departure, state your intention, and then follow whoever comes for you. Your power animal can accompany you at all times.

My intention is to find a teacher who will help me in my issues of sexual health. When you find them, ask your teacher how they will work with you and what you can do for them. When you hear the return beat on the drumming tape, come fully back into your body.

The teacher(s) you meet in this journey will instruct you in various aspects of sexuality. They will meet you where you are and help you with sexual wounds, barriers, inhibitions, and blocks. They will also teach you the meaning of sacred sexuality, the ancient ways and paths.

Teachers have a wonderful sense of humor and may help you overcome shyness or bashfulness with bawdy humor or gentle whimsy. They will help you reconnect to your ecstatic self, which will bring you into alignment both with your physical body and with the Earth. These kinds of teachings are extremely intimate and are found within all sacred traditions of becoming one with the beloved. My advice is to keep these journeys as your private spiritual practice; use reticence when discussing them. If you are in a group dedicated to sacred space, then the container may hold the depth of these kinds of journeys. These relationships are sacred and should be treated as such. Ecstasy is imbedded within shamanic practice. These teachings are profound and will help you heal and grow into your ecstatic self.

Here is a list of questions for you to explore. Take your time and write the answers in your journal. You can take any of these questions and journey to your teachers or power animals.

What is the current state of my sexual life?
What is the current state of my creative life?
What do my dreams tell me about my sexuality?
What was I taught about sex?
What was I taught about marriage?
What was my first sexual experience? How did I feel about it—pleasured, liked, loved, hated, rejected, loathed, lusted after, scared, hurt, bored, funny, pathetic, fabulous?
What was the impact of that first experience? What decisions/beliefs did I form from that first sexual experience, if any?
What is my sexual wound?
What are my sexual addictions?
Can I differentiate between my sexual energy and my partner's?
How do I feel about menstrual or moon-times, my own or my lover's?
Do I feel shame about sexuality?
How do I feel about self-pleasuring? What was I told regarding self-pleasuring?
Do I orgasm? Alone? With a partner?
What do I like sexually? What don't I like? Am I adventurous? Safe?

Do I speak frankly regarding my sexual wishes and boundaries?

Am I happy with my sensual life, whether or not I'm dating or married? How would I like my sexual life to be?

What relationship does spirit have with my sexuality? How would I like this to change, if at all?

How do I feel about lesbians, gays? Why?

What might my next step be to empower myself sexually?

Within these questions lie the textured feelings, desires, hidden agendas, fears, and longings of your sensuality. By diving into this pool you will go to depths you did not know you possessed. By incorporating your shamanic work with a teacher or power animal in this process you will be surprised how much they can help you with healing your sexual self. Doing this work will bring the sacred back into the word "sex." This is what we have lost and need to regain in order to connect with one another as souls, instead of just as bodies.

Journey to Power Animals to request a Ritual of Healing

20min

You can pick an issue, abuse or sexual problem and work with your Animal ally on it. The Power Animals are a great source of nurturing, healing and help with these issues. They may even give you a healing within the journey.

For this particular journey ask the Power Animal to give you a ritual to do to heal your issue. Then create and do the ritual. Give thanks to the spirits.

Initiation through Early Childhood Abuse

There is another very important factor in considering the value of adversity. In all mystery traditions and indigenous cultures, initiation is grueling. Many who go for the higher forms of initiation do not make it; they die. Their soul will have to wait until the next incarnation, to pick up the thread where they left off in training. One of the most important aspects of any initiation rite is the act of courage. The ability to endure and persevere beyond what we think is humanly possible has always been one of the most critical challenges facing an initiate.

Anyone who has undergone childhood sexual, physical, or emotional assault and lived has been initiated and is deemed victorious in passing the test of courage. They are people who have withstood and maintained their life against all odds. This is a high mark of courage in one so young and vulnerable. However, personal initiations do not have to be endured through physical or sexual suffering, although suffering is the key to many initiations. In our Western culture, initiations come upon us like lightning strokes, unlooked for and out of the blue.

We all undergo a personal journey toward integration and wholeness. We have been wounded sexually or in relationship at some point in our lifetime. The unraveling of our story and the pain found there can lead us to discovering new territory and opening up a dialogue with self and spiritual beings.

The spiritual beings work in conjunction with us to help us along the entire journey. They never leave us even if we feel we lose touch with them through overwhelm, grief, anger, fear, or denial. When we submerge into the black depths, the spirits are with us. When we come up for air, they are with us. The spiritual beings are supremely able to cope with and bring about our healing. We can rely on them.

Chapter Ten

Men's Mysteries: Reconnecting to Soul

Men today are very confused about their roles in our shifting gender paradigm. Since we have lost our male mysteries and ceremonies, men have been drifting without spiritual help for a very long time. With the advent of the men's movement, many man are experiencing the support, adventure, and lure of a masculine energy field. They are discovering that time spent with other men is integral to their sense of manhood. Most importantly, they are bringing back the male rituals and ceremonies within a spiritual context.

When boys are born into the world, they enter a very different paradigm than women do. They are born into a culture and social structure that venerates the power, abilities, and talents of men. Men are found throughout the upper echelons of science, arts, politics, economics, and religion. Men can become kings, presidents, dictators, or rulers. In fact, the God of this world is made in *his* image. A boy is born with a divine right to be all that he can be. It is expected of him.

Who Am I?

But despite the rights and privileges inherent in being born male today, there is missing critical information that men need to become whole. At some point it may become obvious that they do not know who they are or how to be a man in our society. So within the high-status jobs and paychecks, men may find they are playing a game. The game is, "Let's pretend I know who I am, what I am doing, and who I am supposed to be as a man."

Men have lost their mysteries. To a large degree this came with the dissolution of the traditional extended-family system in the face of the industrial revolution. The men of today lost touch with their fathers because Dad was always at work providing for the family. Boys grew up isolated from men and male elders. This creates a large gap of information in a man's soul—if he has no role model to show him the traits, talents, gifts, and secrets of men, how will he discover them?

The loss of connection to the father could have been remedied through connection and relationship with a larger group of male mentors. But because of our isolated single-family systems, the loss of community relations, and the daily absence of grandparents who now usually live separate from the younger generations (in most white households, at least), this avenue was generally not available for men. So, boys grew to men without the support critical for their souls' nourishment, testing, and grounding. They had to rely on serendipitous external circumstances for initiation.

Life will initiate boys into men. Today many boys get initiated by other boys, usually through brutality and without honor. Gather men in a group and ask them about growing up, and they will share with you some hair-raising experiences. Mention high school or college, and every single one of them will share a horror story of one kind or another. The abuse ranges from casual cruelty to full-on beatings. Stories include getting heads dunked down toilets, being spat at in the face, being dragged literally through shit by older boys, being tied up and blindfolded, then dropped in the middle of a city. Gang beatings. The stories are endless.

Young Warrior Natures

Young men being raised without strong male guidance will use their natural warrior-like energies in any way they choose. If there is no father or other male figures holding them firmly, there natural rebellious energies may well be directed toward destruction. This gets them into trouble with the law and can negatively influence the course of their lives. Today, many outreach programs are addressing this dilemma for at-risk youths. Much more help is still needed.

Within most indigenous societies, this upsurgence of adolescent male testosterone is recognized and channeled into positive and creative directions through tests, training, and skill-building. Without these containers, endorsed and enforced by the culture and upheld by the status of adult males, we can see where and how this energy can be misdirected.

By guiding this volatile energy into rites-of-passage initiations, the boys are given a taste of pain, suffering, and the endurance necessary to become a man. By suffering themselves, they understand pain. This gives men a healthy respect for inflicting pain on someone else, be it a friend or enemy. One who has suffered greatly will be hesitant to put another through the same, unless they have to.

To bring pain and suffering as a personal experience into a sacred container—as an initiation—teaches the initiated one about the "sacred male" or the divine principles inherent within the souls of men. It is of critical importance that men gather and reclaim their rituals and initiate each other and their sons. It is up to men to teach their sons the proper use of power.

What's the Difference between Girls and Boys?

In order for men and women to gain an understanding of each other and how we differ, we have to look at how our historical, social, cultural, political, and economic status reflect our gender roles and norms. In American society, men and women are socialized into two very different roles. Thus we communicate in two very distinct ways.

Deborah Tannen's book, *You Just Don't Understand*, lays out the female and male patterns that start at the beginning of life. She tells us that boys play outside in groups. The groups are large and have an internal hierarchical structure. The groups play against each other and there are "winner's" and "loser's." There is one group leader who gives orders and makes up elaborate rules. He makes the rules stick and this gives him status. The leader will resist advice, proposals or options from other boys. The way other boys get attention or jockey for status is to tell stories, sidetrack conversations or games, or by challenging the stories and jokes of others. Boys will boast of their prowess, their wins, even their hurts if this brings status within the group context.

Girls are very different. Girls have best friends, and play together in small groups. Within their group dynamic intimacy is the foundational element. Girls games are inclusive and everyone gets a turn. Girls do not give orders, they express their desires. Girls who are loud, bold or ask directly for what they want may be called "bossy." (Pgs. 43, 44)

These social trainings create a built-in one-up, one-down, power-over scenario. A man will tend to jockey for a dominant position in relationship, and a woman will tend to give it to him. This dynamic is the *socialized* gender norm we are dealing with. Until very recently men have grown up in a cultural and social environment, endorsed by the church, that casts women in the second-class roles of nurturers and caretakers of men. In all other positions women are still typically portrayed (for the most part) in diminished or sexually derogatory ways in marketing, movies, and within our social strata.

    As a boy grows into manhood and feels pressured to assume the role cast him by his family, peers, and community, he learns the art of retreat. This alienates and isolates him from other men. Because of the dominator positioning, many men do not have deep and abiding friendships with men, and many say they feel safer with women as friends. This places men in a very precarious position—they are caught in a competitive dynamic with other men (whom they usually do not trust) or in a male-female "friendship" that is fraught with its own difficulties and built-in power-over scenarios. This can be a very tenuous and painful position.

    Adding to this, the relationships between men and women are changing. Since the advent of the women's rights movement in the sixties, the ever-widening ripples have reached the mainstream. Men are being directly affected by women struggling to emerge within their loving relationships and the job market. Women have joined the work force in ever-growing numbers to increase the family income, and they are consequently requesting men to take equal responsibilities for the children and the household duties. Women are finding they cannot be a supermom, a career woman, and a loving wife all at the same time. More and more men are seen grocery shopping, jogging, and out in public with a baby strapped to them. Gender roles are shifting, and within the role reversals both men and women are learning about how the other half lives.

This dynamic, shifting paradigm forces men to question their socialization process. Many men do not want to uphold the dominator role they've learned—with each other or with women—but they don't know how to create a new and less biased form of relating.

The Men's Class

The men's class that I teach, *Journey to the Sacred Male*, opens up the discussion among men of what it means to be a man in today's changing society. The men are (mainly) relieved to let down the pretense that they have erected around themselves regarding who they are as men. In fact, when asked, almost every man cannot say or does not know what it means to be a man. They neither know nor understand what is expected of them in relation to other men, let alone who they are or how they "should" act with women. This isn't a surprise, given the rapid changes that have taken place regarding traditional and contemporary gender roles.

With the class focus on developing a spiritual practice, many men experience their first communication with spiritual beings. Using the shamanic journey to access the spiritual worlds, they develop their relationships with teachers who are committed to helping them learn the ways of the sacred male. The spirits give the men plenty of information, teachings, directives, and gifts. Speaking and working directly with spiritual beings opens up worlds of beauty, delight, and adventure.

For many men this class is the first time they develop a personal spiritual discipline with the intention of bringing the sacred into their daily lives. The spirits begin to come into the men's dreams and show up in synchronistic events. Some men experience mystical phenomena. At one point or another the men realize that the work they are doing with the spiritual beings is authentic. This realization sends shock waves into their constructed worldview and challenges it. This is one of the first struggles—to accept spiritual reality will mean rethinking their concepts of reality.

The Spiritual Crisis of a Young Priest

One of the male students had undergone a spiritual crisis at nineteen when he was in a seminary studying to be a priest. He discovered that the priests were having sexual relations with each other, and that this was acceptable behavior--but hidden under the church's cloak of secrecy and denial. He was shattered.

That night he left the seminary and stayed the night in a church graveyard and experienced a profound crisis during which he saw and heard the spirits all night long. He was lying with his back against huge tree, and was assaulted with loud voices and visions all the night through. He said that he felt the tree was the only reason he lived that night.

When morning dawned the supernatural phenomena dissolved. He got up and staggered toward the graveyards gate...where he saw two nuns sitting on a bench gazing up at him. They had extraordinary blue eyes. He felt a jolt of power, and fear coursed through him--he left hurriedly. He found out later that the graveyard was a "Nun's graveyard"-- and that since this was an all male seminary it was impossible for him to see two nuns that morning.

This experience shook up his worldview so much he pushed it deep down. Soon after he left the priesthood and became a psychologist. He was drawn to shamanism, yet he was truly terrified of doing this kind of work for fear that he would relive his previous experience and "crack up."

He had wonderfully deep shamanic journeys, but because of his psychological training he negated his experiences through his fears of splitting, psychosis, and the like. Even so, his journeys became stronger and more beautiful. Many times he would come back to the group looking transformed and radiant—the energy he emanated was tangible to all of us in the circle. The messages he received during his journeys were profound and healing. But the richer his journeys, the more frightened he became. To his credit he showed up for class every week. But after these profound experiences he would diminish them by labeling them neurotic and then processing his fear. He just could not get over the hump to believe that he was not going nuts but was actually accessing spiritual realities.

Dismemberment: Out with the Old & In with the New

The spirits took compassion on him and gave him a healing. They gave him a shamanic dismemberment by coming to him in the dreamtime and severing his head from his neck. He saw his brains being eaten away, and although he experienced no pain, this profoundly disgusted him. Then he was given a new head and brains. This is classic shamanic work. In this way the spirits took compassion on him and his overworked brain, which was trying to meld rigid psychological models to include a shamanic view much vaster in scope.

They simply took out his old brains and gave him new ones. It is a metaphor—he did not experience this brain removal in his ordinary life—but it is also a reality in that a true shamanic healing took place. This dismemberment got rid of outmoded patterns and beliefs and allowed him to interpret information differently. It opened his ability to accept spirit in new ways other than the psychological model that tells him he is experiencing psychosis rather than direct revelations.

Rites-of-Passage Rituals

The main work for the men is to reestablish the male mysteries lost to them. Through this process a direct connection to spirit happens, usually through the gateway of nature, spiritual practices, or dreaming. As men remember what it means to be a sacred male, they also learn to honor the mother as the sacred fount of all life, partially through meeting their own inner female.

Some men in the class admitted that although they understood the women's movement for equal rights and agree with it, they still find deep within them that they want their female partners to take care of them, to nurture them in ways that go beyond a lover's role.

One man in an undisguised exhibition of complete honesty stated that it was difficult giving up the rights and privileges inherently granted him just by being born male. Although he understood the discrepancy and the pain it caused women, he still struggled to "allow" or "grant" women the same rights. He even understood, after stating this, that he was still operating under the premise that this right was *his* to grant to women, not a divine right of equality among genders.

One of the important rituals for the men is the work of reclaiming and taking responsibility for their lives through a rites-of-passage ritual, "Leaving the Mother." In most instances men didn't separate from their mother in a clean way. It is the father's duty to take the boy at a certain age, bring him into the masculine world, and initiate him. Not having this rite of passage produces fall-out in men's personal lives. Since there was no line of demarcation of leaving their mother and becoming a man, they found they transferred onto their dates, spouses, or other females their unresolved "mother stuff."

The men's class developed this next ritual in co-creation with their helping spirits. The object of the ritual is for the men to take responsibility for their actions regarding the feminine aspect of their world. Ritual, to work, must be filled with the power of the helping spirits. If the men are sincere and filled with the power of spirits, they will succeed in this separating ceremony that enables them to embrace a richer, fuller manhood and to see women with clearer eyes.

Journey to Upper World Teacher 20 min

Request a Rites of Passage Ritual for Releasing the Mother

My intention is to go to the Upper World and ask my teacher for a ritual to, "release my mother in a sacred way." The men's group create, design, plan and enact their ritual together. This is done only by the men and they keep the ritual secret. This is considered an initiation ceremony.

~Healing a Man's Wounded Heart~

During one of the class cycles, I had a dream of seeing a student, whom I'll call Lee, with an old rusty ax buried deep into his heart. As a shamanic practitioner I receive prophetic dreams telling me about my clients, and I have learned to trust and work with them. From a shamanic perspective, the dream showed me that Lee had an old wound regarding matters of the heart, and since he was walking around in the dream, it implied that he had learned to live with it. On meeting with him privately I asked him if I could share my dream content. He readily assented, and I told him what had visited me. When I was finished with the dream I asked him if he had any knowledge of who might have sunk that ax into his heart.

Although he typically shared to a deep level in group (we were working on shadow material in intimate relationships in the men's class), it wasn't until this dream event that he shared his original love wound. He related that sixteen years ago he was completely in love with a girl whom he felt was *"the One."* He had planned to marry her. But shortly into the relationship, she dropped him for a homeless man. This doubly devastated him, affecting him on both emotional and physical levels. He lost weight and the will to work, his self-esteem plummeted, and he fell ill. He underwent "the dark night of the soul" and promised himself that he would never be hurt like that again.

The Vow of the Non-Commitment

He kept that vow; he always left his relationships any time the subject of marriage or commitment came up. He had never connected his non-committal behavior in relationships to that initial wounding. Considering the message within my dream provided a revelation to him.

That is not where the work ended, however. From a shamanic view the dream was not only for information but also for showing me that he had a spiritual wound in his heart. It appeared to me as an ax, but that was a symbol of a spiritual intrusion in his heart region. He was willing for me to do a shamanic extraction process and pull the "ax" out of his chest. We decided to do this at the end of the group cycle, when the men's and women's groups got together to co-create healing ceremonies between the male and female principles.

The ax also signified that Lee had probably suffered soul loss due to the trauma that happened to him sixteen years ago. For his healing ceremony, I asked Lee to bring an ax to the all-day workshop. I was going to create a symbolic forum for Lee's unconscious to open up in order for him to move past his rational mind and to receive the healing. We waited until the end of the day, after the sharing and other ceremonies, when the energy was very charged with love and healing. At that time I shared my dream, and Lee shared his heart-wound story with the group. The group agreed to support him by drumming for the healing ceremony as I did the extraction process.

I carefully tucked the ax deep in his left armpit and told him to go back to that time of betrayal with his beloved. I told him not to let go of the ax until he was ready to let her go as well. His face was wide open and tears shimmered in his eyes. The drummers started a monotonous beat and I called in my healing spirits. I pulled and pulled, the drumming built in tempo, the air became charged with power. I pulled on the ax until suddenly it came free. Lee jerked off the ground and started to weep uncontrollably.

Bury the Hatchet

I did a soul retrieval and brought his soul essence back to him. If a person is not filled with spiritual essence after an extraction, they are wide open for new psychic intrusion to (yet again) lodge in the void. A soul retrieval fills one up with one's own spiritual essence, and then illness cannot take hold. For follow-up work, I instructed Lee to literally bury the hatchet, do a healing forgiveness ceremony, and take personal responsibility for stopping particular behaviors with women, which had become a compulsive way of relating. Since that retreat, he has been in a committed relationship for years and reports that he is working on their connection and intimacy in creative ways.

Chapter Eleven

Women's Mysteries: Where Did They Go?

We are in a time of great change as we leave behind the twentieth century and enter the new millennium. The world is in critical need during this transition. Taking place right now is the long-awaited rebirth of the sacred feminine, which promises to bring balance back into our world. We are actually caught in an evolutionary process, one that has been planned in great detail in the supersensible worlds and has been in play for quite some time.

The spiritual beings who work in concert with Earth consciousness are streaming upon us the energy and love of the divine feminine. We here on Earth must open our soul forces to receive that love. We must receive, move, and integrate this feminine field into our world. The successful rebirth of the divine feminine depends especially on every woman's ability to begin the process of emergence—emergence into a recognition of spiritual gifts, creative power, passion, and life purpose. As women emerge so, too, the divine feminine emerges.

What can women do to help this process? One step is to focus on educating themselves, for within education lies knowledge that leads to expansion and freedom. Start reading! There are literally hundreds of books on the

Goddess traditions, feminist theory, and alternative scriptures that include a mother creator. Get educated about family violence; learn communication skills; do self-esteem and recovery work; find a creative practice that delights you. Reclaim your body through dance, massage, grief work—discover what is offered and available. Attend workshops and take part in women's circles. If there are no women's groups handy, start your own.

Birthing is never an easy time. The time just before birth is critical, fraught with pain, fear, and contractions until the head crowns and the child is born with the mother's last great pushes. Who is willing to help our Earth in her labor pains? Who will greet this feminine force and open to it? The work of men is to anchor their divine masculine principle, which calls the feminine field to blossom.

The second thing a woman must do is to heal her wounds so she can actualize her dreams. A woman's wounds lie not just within her own story, however; her wounds are embedded within a historical, political, and religious context of gender suppression. In order for women to be educated about women's power issues, they need to know when they had power and when they lost it. For most of us in the West, this heritage lies in Europe, and so we go back into prehistory to study the Goddess traditions.

A Male God? Says Who?

Learning about the Goddess in her many forms is one of the most empowering aspects of women's spiritual work today. The Goddess was revered as the Queen of Heaven, and sex and love were worshipped as divine rites. Women were empowered within society and enjoyed high-status positions, such as; priestesses, land owners, and healers.

Anthropologists postulate that the fall of matriarchal cultures was associated with nations that conquered those societies. As the centuries anchored the dominant patriarchal culture, women were recognized and noted as healers, but on a rising and descending wave. In some societies they would rise to prominence, but later were erased by the historical documentation by men.

During the time of Christ, women were acknowledged within the new religion's concepts and defined in much broader terms than Christianity does today. It is suspected the church buried or destroyed from the original holy texts passages that indicated women's more equal status. Many of the alternative creation myths state that the first primal force was woman and all things sprang from her.

It is interesting to see how women were submerged and dismissed, endorsed by the Hebrew and Christian interpretations of an all-male God. Some interesting questions to ask are, "Who interpreted the holy texts and scriptures?" and, "Were they interpreted accurately?" Dion Fortune (1935), the noted initiate of the Golden Dawn, addresses in her book, *The Mystical Qabalah*, the issue of a male-aspected God. She says, "A Goddessless religion is halfway to atheism. In the word Elohim we find the true key. Elohim is translated "God" in both Authorized and Revised Versions of the Holy Scriptures. It really ought to be translated "God and Goddess," for it is a feminine noun with a masculine plural termination affixed..." "And the spirit of the male and female conjoined principles moved upon the surface of the formless, and manifestation took place." (p. 153)

Taking the feminine force out of the word Elohim in the language matrix grants free license to taking women out of the picture globally. Over centuries of obscuring and obliterating women's contributions, gifts, talents, and traditions, mainly through not writing them into the records, women ceased to exist within a historical context except as agents of barter and trade.

The church proclaims there is only a male God. It lessened women's status by editing the Creation Story which makes women evil and sinful. The church established it's hold over the masses by making itself the one and only gateway as pardoner of sins for the heavenly bound sinner. Through this edict it claimed absolute obedience and developed it's all encompassing economic power base.

The Witch Trials

Within the horrific stories surrounding the women accused of witchcraft, we discover that these "witches" were independent, highly skilled women with spiritual gifts who were typically tortured and publicly murdered in barbaric fashions. What happened?

The church elders saw women as competition for their priests in both spiritual counseling and birth control. Within every small village women were practicing as counselors, herbalist's and shamans; they were feared, respected, and honored. Today they would be called professional therapists, doctors, mid-wives. Examination of historical documents reveals that the women who were labeled and stigmatized as "witches" had wide and varied disciplines and abilities such as:

- midwives
- surgeons
- diviner
- physicians
- barbers
- bonesetters
- necromancer
- curser
- gynecologists
- herbalist's
- diagnosticians
- countermagician

If women had thriving practices in villages, towns and cities, then women held enormous power-power that the church wanted. If the church could wrest this power from women and hand it to their priests, they could more fully control the masses.

Also the church had not been totally successful in making Christianity the predominant belief. People who proclaimed to be Christian, nevertheless celebrated the old pagan religious festivals and rites as well. The church could not easily eradicate the folk-people's lingering love of nature spirits.

The church leaders also wanted to wipe out the shamanic traditions that women were practicing with so much success. How could they attack both women and shamanism (paganism) and still be supported within each town? In order to bring women under its domination, the church had to make its nefarious campaign a religious one. They needed to connect women's shamanic gifts with the idea that they were acting against Christian dictates. To do this they attacked the old religion.

Demonizing the Nature Spirits

The church wrested power from the Goddess traditions by changing the creation myths to make Women evil. (There are Garden creation myths that predates our Genesis by seven centuries in which men and women are equal) By taking the Feminine out of the language matrix, and rewriting the creation stories to diminish the status of women, the church subverted women's power and her Goddess. As a strategy, it worked very well.

Now, the church viewed Pan, the overriding male nature spirit as Christ's main opposition. By using the same strategy, they renamed Pan the devil making him Christ's arch fiend.

To attack women the church officials wrote the *Malleus Maleficarum*, (The Witches Hammer), a manual used to legitimize the witch-hunts. The Witches Hammer stated that all witchcraft comes from women's insatiable carnal lust. By subverting Pan into the devil, and linking women and the Devil together sexually, the church in one fell blow made a bid to seize power from women and shamanic practices.

The witch hunts were created just as some wars today are created-for control and power. Anyone could proclaim a woman a "witch" and she would be taken away from her family and practice. The witch hunts were fueled by hysteria, lies, jealousies, petty feuds and revenge.

Since the church had already stated women were sinful because of their sexual appetites and were in league with the devil, there was not much room in that set-up for a fair trial. A woman accused of witchcraft would be thrown into a filthy prison, kept isolated, starved, stripped and searched, had her genitals and breasts fondled, she could be raped, threatened for sexual favors, raped and murdered--all while waiting for her trial.

After thousands of executions over three centuries, women internalized that their bodies and physical functions were evil, that their sexuality was evil, and that their natural spiritual gifts of healing were also evil. Women learned to become invisible. Under this continual suppression, women got the message. They stopped sharing their spirit gifts with anyone, even friends, and certainly didn't talk about them.

They hid their bodies in fear and shame. They learned not to talk back, not to voice opinions, not to breast feed in public, until by the nineteenth century the sexually repressed, passive, neurotic women that Freud saw in his waiting rooms were born.

By eradicating women's voices, patriarchy has eradicated women's traditions. Women do not remember their gifts because their gifts have not been recognized within our culture. Women's silence has been dearly bought through threat, fear, and murder.

Women may well wonder, when they are pursuing a goal out in the world, why they will suddenly encounter the terror of being killed welling up within their psyches. Bringing this information to light within a group context lays the necessary foundation for addressing this cellular fear.

Accepting Spirit Gifts and Discovering Life Purpose

In the Alchemy class, most women had spiritual gifts: hands that would get hot (healing abilities); psychic abilities—seeing, divining, clairaudiance, clairvoyance and prophetic dreams. These women had extraordinary gifts, and they rarely if ever talked about it—to anyone—let alone used their talents.

Until we broached the topic in class of women having spiritual gifts, they really had not given it too much attention. They did not know they were keeping silent about it. This is how insidiously our cultural negation of female gifts and traditions affects women. They don't even realize they are being repressed because they have grown up in a cultural model that accepts the silence of women (and their shamanic talents) as normal.

Our spiritual gifts define our life purpose. If we do not have a cultural container for women's wisdom ways, how can we identify female gifts? If our culture denies this information, through writing women out of history, women must self-educate. For anyone, regardless of gender, identifying our spiritual gifts will point us toward what we are to give to the world.

We have to access this information. Otherwise we can just drift from job to job, filled with frustration and impotence. If women gain an understanding of their life purpose and go forward toward manifesting destiny, they may encounter that cellular fear that feels like they will be killed for their beliefs or for being seen.

Many women are manifesting their life purposes, but a great many women are still floating in personal limbo. Circles provide a safe place in which to start talking about gifts of spirit and the historical punishment of women for their sexual and spiritual gifts.

Facing Fear

Moving toward one's life purpose can activate tremendous fear and resistance. The shadow can rise, pointing out unconscious motivations and desires. One of the most important acts for women is facing their worst fears and choosing to go through them. Since women are repressed globally, this process of facing fears needs to be ritualized within a spiritual and group context. If the ritual is completed successfully, women will no longer project their bright shadow (their own power) onto a man or someone else to hold for them; they will generate and promote their own life purpose. Addressing deep inner fears within a ceremony helped by spiritual beings is a rare opportunity for cellular healing.

Women who move through their own challenges in relation to power will no longer be content to be in a "power-over" or "power-under" scenario—they will have the strength to take creative action and make new choices.

Journeys for Women and Men

Journey to Teacher in UW and Face Your Fear 30min

Your intention is to journey to the Upper World and meet your teacher. Ask your teacher to show your greatest fears, then choose whether or not you are willing to go through them. Typically the teachers present a number of scenarios.

Fear stops us from expanding, exploring, taking adventures and side roads in life. This is an extremely powerful journey, if you choose to face and experience the fears that are presented you will benefit greatly. You will have a deeper understanding of what fears are "running you unconsciously." This can bring up fear, tears and grief, so please allow for plenty of time to process the emotions. You can journal or draw pictures, write a story or even journey back into certain scenarios that you wish to explore. This is the work of the deep self and the unconscious. This journey may point to past-life trauma as well.

Journey to Teacher in UW

Ask to be Shown a Past Life 20min

Your intention is to go to the Upper World find your teacher and ask to be taken to a Past-Life (or lives) that holds a key to your present healing and development. Many times you will be shown or experience an incident that holds a great deal of emotional power that is directly linked to a present day problem, pattern or trauma. If you chose you can re-experience that life event. Then ask your teacher;

How is this past-life incident *linked* to what problem, pattern or trauma in my present life?
In what way does this past life incident hold a key to my present development?
What needs to be healed or brought into balance from this past life in order to free me in my present life?
What kind of ritual can be done to bring resolution and healing to this issue?

When you return from your journey take some time to process, write down and draw any relevant information, "aha" revelations, or key thoughts and feelings. Then create and do the ritual that was given. You will want to look for results from the ritual work in the life issue.

Psychopomp Work

To do any work of helping the Ancestors, or spirits of the deceased "cross over to the other side" is called psychopomp work. Many of us are capable of doing this work in conjunction with the helping spirits and teachers. Some people have a definite "calling" to this type of healing work.

Journey to A Witch and Help Them Cross-Over 30min

This is a beautiful and intimate journey you can do alone or within a group context. The intention is to travel back in time to help a witch-female or male-at the time of their tribulation and trial. You are to ask your teacher or Power Animal to seek a Healer from the times of the trials. You are to ask to see them as they were children, how they grew up and when and how their spiritual gifts manifested. Go forward into the future and see how they put their gifts to use in the world. Then see when they got accused and tried for witchcraft.

You may very well view atrocities, but you have the help of the spirit allies and angels to do this very necessary work. Be with them in their imprisonment; comfort them, pray and ask that the Great Ones enter their dreams to effuse them with strength and endurance. At the time of their "transition" or death, help them cross over. Pray strongly for them. Help them into the "light" or to the next level with support and love. Some people report that the "witch" becomes a strong teacher and protecting spirit for them.

Journey to a War Vet and Help them Cross Over-30min

This journey arose spontaneously in the men's group one night. A man came back sobbing with the information from his teachers that this psychopomp work is critically needed. Rituals can be done in group for these men who died in battle.

Women's Ritual for Healing the Grief of Abortion

Before the chapter on women's work ends I want to address a most grievous wound many women carry- abortions or miscarriages.

One of the women in the group who I will call Elaine, was in a repetitive pattern of dating men who were abusing her emotionally and physically. She knew that she was pulling these men to her, but she could not understand why. As her soul work deepened, she allowed an old wound to surface to consciousness. She shared that when she was a teenager she fell in love and got pregnant. The boy, on finding out she was pregnant dropped her immediately and allowed no further contact. She decided to have an abortion and did so in secret without help from her family or friends.

This issue was never dealt with emotionally, as she discounted and stuffed the experience, and just got on with life. Fifteen years later, however, she brought up and relived the guilt, disappointment, anger and deep sadness of losing her lover and her baby. She also shared that she had repeating dreams of her baby girl coming to her...these dreams caused her deep distress.

Elaine discovered "the pattern" of why she kept drawing to her abusive men-all of whom were reminiscent of her high school lover. She realized because she had never resolved her anger, grief and pain, she unconsciously continued to draw the same type of man as he was. She kept repeating the pattern that her soul wished to heal.

Elaine came to understand that she was "holding on to her baby" by not fully grieving the loss of this soul. She received a ritual in her journeywork to enact at the retreat in the women's rites of passage work. She was to make a cloth baby doll, cover it with her prayers and menstrual blood, and send it to the Other Side. This is psychopomp ritual work. (A psychopomp is one who help the dead or dying cross over) We incorporated the help of the other women to hold her ritual work. As the women loved her greatly, they were eager to help "hold" her intention.

When it was time, the women sat on the floor forming a long chain with a women sitting in front of her between her open legs. We started to sing and rattle and the women started singing and swaying, leaning back into each other, then swaying forward. The intention was to focus their wills in alignment with Elaine's as she "pushed her baby's soul" into the *Other World* with the power of the helping spirits, and let her go.

Elaine sat in the front of the long chain, nestled between a women's legs, swaying forward and leaning back fully into the women behind her, all the while holding her baby and rocking it. She began to weep and wail. The tears streamed out of her eyes, and the energy rose. The building tension could be felt, the spirits were ringed round us, and at the point of power, Elaine lifted the doll to the spiritual worlds. She wept and wailed while all the women gathered around her and comforted her with healing words and prayers. Later Elaine buried the doll in a by a tree she loved.

The tension within Elaine's soul had to be ex-pressed into outward action. Elaine integrated this ritual and this allowed her to come to conscious understanding of where her relationship patterns sprang from. And make creative choices in relationship consciously.

Chapter Twelve

The Third Gender: Reconstructing the Cosmic Heart

Let's take a look at how our gender roles have been constructed within our Western culture. The classifying of gender variance will also be viewed through different cultures, indigenous traditions, and spiritual roles. This material provides just an overview of gender variance, sexual roles, and societal norms; it is not meant to be a full accounting of such a complex topic. This discussion is offered as education about the problems and misconceptions that form the ongoing Western process regarding sexual diversity.

Who Wrote the Rules?

The first thing we must address before talking about specifics in gender diversity is the cultural container regarding gender and sexuality we have created here in America. For the most part, we have internalized pleasurable, healthy sexual relations as dirty, evil, and shameful. This is due largely to the teachings the Christian church formulated for us. As with all things we are forbidden, sex became a most desired fruit. Adding insult to injury, sex is a fun, downright ecstatic pastime. It took the church centuries of applied fear and force to convince us of the idea that sex is a sin.

By proclaiming sex out of wedlock sinful while declaring moral, upstanding individuals to be free from its taint and lure, the church officials created both the moral majority and an enormous sexual shadow for the culture. This kind of repression, supported by a religious institution with such massive power to form belief systems and control people's behaviors, creates widespread sexual shame and shadow material.

Anne Wilson Schaef in her book *Escape from Intimacy* comments on contemporary issues regarding sexuality and addiction in the church, "I believe that many of our most outspoken leaders of organized religion are themselves sexual addicts. ... Those things we are obsessed with and we try to repress become obsessions. Those things that we try to repress usually find their way out and frequently we act out in ways that are confusing for ourselves and those around us." (p. 39)

The sexual activity of priests has been covered up for centuries under the dual cloaks of denial and secrecy. In the beginnings of Christianity there were no hard and fast laws regarding the marital status of Christ's followers; many of the original disciples were already married. Many popes fathered sons who in turn became popes, and many men were married before becoming priests.

A.W. Richard Sipe, a retired, ordained Roman Catholic priest, blew the whistle on sexual activities within the church in his 1990 book, "*A Secret World*." He states, "The justification for male superiority and the introduction of evil into the cosmic system via sex both hinge on the church's view of women. According to church tradition, the only good woman is silent, sexless, and subservient. My study of celibacy has left no doubt that this attitude is still alive and well in clerical circles." (p. 30)

A Secret World opens up the cloistered lives of priests who are torn between leading a celibate life and following their sensual desires. This conflict leads some of them into sexual experiences with other men, children, adolescent girls and boys, and nuns and other women. Sipe writes, "Ironically, the legislation against marriage and sexual activity for clerics produced two notable side effects in the church: 1) an increase in the transgressions against chastity and the rearticulated rule of celibacy; and 2) a continuing degradation of women." (p. 39)

Although sexuality within the church was an ongoing and continual problem, it wasn't until the twelfth century when legislation against marriage and sexual activity for clerics took force that the sexual shadow projection magnified and birthed the beginning of the witch-hunts.

Suddenly, priests indulging in any form of sexual release had gone against church rule and sinned against God. The only way for these men to continue within this rigid framework was to stop all sexual activity or to split their consciousness and hide their sexuality.

Priests were expected to subdue their intrinsic passions for the love of God, for a doctrine of enforced chastity and celibacy. Celibacy is not for everyone, and it is a very difficult path even for those who choose it freely. That every man who entered the priesthood should adopt such a rigorous role under oath was perilous at best. Priests who could not overcome their sexual drives were told by their superiors that is was better to meet their needs than to give up the priesthood—some were told privately to take care of themselves or to "take a housekeeper." Sexual relations between priests were not usually addressed but were consciously overlooked.

The church, which turned a blind eye to the ongoing sexual activities of its members, endorsed denial and secrecy while publicly declaring their chosen ones free of the taint of sex. But, in spite of the oath of celibacy, the issues of sexuality within the church became more problematic. Although many priests followed the dictates of the church with good intentions, others had outside affairs with women, some fathered children, and some turned their sexual attractions onto their brothers.

The church surely realized that celibacy, the sublimation of sexual drive, was not an attainable goal for all priests. Instead of taking this under consideration and seeking other alternatives for releasing sexual tension, the church dove more deeply into the split of denial and secrecy. It could not address directly the homosexual relations priests were having with each other, as this would point to an internal failure within the institution of the church itself. Instead, it projected the blame for this failure onto women.

By blaming women for the priests' failed sexual vows, the church publicly side-stepped internal issues. The sublimation of the priests' sexual drives was supposed to birth divine love and creative service in God's name. Instead, it birthed a holocaust for women. The witch-hunts were the result of a profound lack of responsibility and duplicity on the part of the church superiors.

The church, by labeling women as sexually insatiable, inferior, evil liars, emotionally and morally weak, prepared the groundwork for murder. By killing thousands of women, the church tried to manipulate priests away from the lures of sexuality and to overthrow women's wisdom paths, all at once. But those priests who were looking for a sexual outlet, regardless of doctrine, were going to find it. Today the church still denies homosexual behaviors among priests, despite the documented case studies. The church, supposedly based on Christ's doctrine of love and forgiveness, during the witch trials laid a corrupt foundation of repression, degradation, and murder of thousands of women and their families, thus taking for its bedfellow the very things Christ spoke against—the sins of deception, hatred, hypocrisy, evil, and murder.

Many people today are unaware of how we came to the negative labeling of our sexual natures and the repression of women. Many are spiritually and socially apathetic; they see the hypocrisy of the church and equate it with the Christ Consciousness and throw it all overboard. The teachings of Christ have little or nothing to do with the institution of the church and its acts. This is not to say that there aren't many sincere and devout people—leaders, priests, and nuns— within its context.

But as Richard Sipe reminds us in his second book, *Sex, Priests and Power,* " The parameters of the conflict are not limited to a relatively few men who may or may not practice the celibacy they profess. The power of Catholic priests and the sexual reasoning of Christian tradition have implications for life on this planet, including the issues of population growth, gender and racial equality, and understanding the nature of human sexuality. The salient questions are not about the theoretical preferences, venerable traditions or sacred opinions. The questions are practical struggles for truth, which affect people's lives and the future of the planet." (p. xvi)

The cover-up within the church needs to be faced squarely and understood if we are to ascertain the effects our upbringing in a Christian society has had on our gender relations. This split between men and women was engineered by the edited "holy texts" and strict dictates. If we allow a spiritual institution originally founded on the laws of love and forgiveness to get away with murder, what does that say about our culture? If we accept the lie and pretend it does not exist, what does it say about us personally? Through ignorance or pretense, we collude with the church by default. We agree to it because of our silence. This negative contract limits and binds our society. Within this context, we can consider how men's and women's gender roles are enacted in our society today.

Men's and Women's Gender Roles

By naming men the superior authority and women the second sex, the church has constructed restrictive male and female roles. By denying the homosexual participants within its fold, the church disavows and denies homosexuals in society. Therefore our society expects everyone to fit into either the all-male or the all-female role. Too bad our gender roles don't match our cultural hero myths. In a culture where we glorify those self-willed, creative individuals who cut their own trail through civilization's brush, we do not recognize and celebrate this same trait when it comes to gender variance.

This rigid set of gender roles and the massive negation of homosexual activity within religious institutions create a corresponding sexual shadow that society plays out. If we have erotic fantasies that go outside the "me man, you woman" sexual-pairing scenario, we can feel shame, anger, and resentment. This repression leads to a shadow market of pornography, where we find anything goes. Pornography and sexual violence can be viewed as the acting out of our collective sexual shadow.

Within the secrecy of our sexual fantasies, many of us will at one time or another think about making love with someone of the same sex. Engaging in sexual play with someone of the same gender is accepted in many societies as a normal experimentation for youths. It is nothing to worry about. People who feel they are called to live a same-gender-loving lifestyle are integrated into the societies. But in our current sexual environment, we Americans usually demonstrate no such flexibility. We turn same-gender sex, lesbians, and gays into the enemy, and with that label we persecute and even kill them.

We can readily understand this as we hear the multitude of stories about sexual abuse within families, the silence regarding priests' sexual relations with each other, and the many sex scandals of psychologists, doctors, educators—up to our highest office, the U.S. presidency. I think it's safe to say that one of America's spiritual lessons is to heal the collective sexual wound.

The Great American Hero: Bustin' the Cowboy Myth

Here in America we grew up with the idealized cowboy myth, popularized by John Wayne, of the masculine, rough-'n'-ready man who rides the range. What was the life of a lone cowboy or rancher really like? The Kinsey report, a massive survey of American male sexual behavior taken in the 1940s states;

There is a fair amount of sexual contact among the older males in Western rural areas. It is a type of homosexuality which was probably common among pioneers and outdoor men in general. Today it is found among ranchmen, cattlemen, prospectors, lumbermen, and farming groups in general—among groups that are virile, physically active. These are men who have faced the rigors of nature in the wild. They live on realities and on a minimum of theory. Such a background breeds the attitude that sex is sex, irrespective of the nature of the partner.

Cowboys were men who adapted their sexuality to suit their needs and their isolated life style. We have witnessed same-gender coupling within our religious systems, military groups, and cowboy myths--isn't it strange how it is always covered up? By coming out of denial and speaking directly about same-sex pairing, we will start the process of disintegrating our sexual shame and shadow blame-game. By acknowledging sexual liaisons between people of the same gender, perhaps we can begin the work of normalizing and acceptance, allowing each individual to experience the personal freedom suggested within our Bill of Rights.

Since we in the West have negated, denied, and stigmatized gender variance and homosexual behavior, we do not have an understanding of the gifts, talents, or spiritual purpose of people who enter life in such incarnations. Thus, we will look to other cultures and spiritual traditions to see how they integrate gender variance and what its spiritual gifts may be.

Native Americans and Gender Roles

If we look at the culture of the first Americans, the peoples who lived here for centuries before white settlers, we see cultural differences in gender roles. Many native cultures do not have such rigid boundaries shaping men and women as we have imposed in our American values. We find that men and women and gender varieties in between were accepted within their societies. They held a place of dignity and honor while bringing the community special spiritual gifts. Some of these people are homosexual, but many are not. This means there are men and women who, although they have attributes of both genders, do not necessarily lead a gay or lesbian lifestyle.

To address gender diversity, the Navaho have delineated five gender variances: the female gender, the male gender, the Nadleeh (hermaphrodite), the masculine-female gender (male-identified female), and the feminine-male gender (female-identified male). Navaho gender variance fits within their social, spiritual, and cultural traditions, which we as Westerners may not understand.

Two-Spirit Person

In other Native traditions another term to denote a person who combines the roles of both genders within one body is "berdache" or a "Two-Spirit Person." The honor and respect that these positions once held within native cultures is in some dispute now that the Western mindset has infiltrated. But perhaps in reviewing how different cultures integrated the two-spirit people and their spiritual gifts we can rescue a wisdom tradition we have helped destroy.

The Gatekeepers

In Africa, the Dagora tribe has gatekeepers. Gatekeepers hold a special place in the community and are believed to have rare spiritual gifts very similar to two-spirit people within Native-American traditions. Their gifts relate to spiritual work and gender reconciliation. Gatekeepers are also the keepers of the mysteries of the universe.

Gatekeepers within the Dagora tradition do not talk within their society about their sexuality—their sexual relations are considered no one's business. As with the Native-American concept of two-spirited people, the way of being is independent of sexual preferences.

The Spiritual Gifts of the Third Gender

Two-spirit people—the third gender—contain aspects of both genders inside of them; therefore they stand on the edges, the borders, the crossroads between worlds. They are the rim walkers. What are the gifts of such an orientation?

The gifts are varied and complex depending on which tradition they practice and the personality of the individual. Historically, two-spirit people enacted rituals, presided over ceremonies, created sacred art of high degree, served as mediators between genders, practiced in-between gender roles. Some were shamans; all were mysterious.

Two-spirit people are often found in the creative and healing arts, as artists, counselors, psychologists, priests, nuns, doctors, shamanic practitioners, or alternative healers. Considering the extremely gifted men and women in the arts and especially in Hollywood and Broadway, we see that not only have some two-spirited people carved a niche for themselves but they are also accepted within the wider and more flexible conditions of the arts. But depending on their personality and spiritual path, a two-spirit person will go where they are called, whether that leads to a life as a teacher, lawyer, scientist, engineer, doctor, parent, mystic, or holy person.

How can we apply this information to our Western culture in creative ways? Given the spiritual implications of two-spirit people, we could guess that they are beloved of divinity; they resemble the androgynous Christ, who was also both male and female. By educating ourselves we can lift off the yoke of ignorance that locks us into gender roles we did not choose. As adults with personal power we can choose to be flexible, inclusive, and loving toward others and ourselves for being different.

Spiritual Crisis as the Consequences of Suppression

One reason for the decline in the power and spirituality of the church stems from its ongoing failure to recognize the problems of enforced celibacy and the suppression of the spiritual gifts of women and men who fit within the third-gender classification. Through its history of negating and even murdering with conscious intent a large part of humanity, the church defeats itself and its purpose in society as a spiritual leader of love and forgiveness.

It is no exaggeration to say that Western society is in spiritual crisis. In addition to learning more about the role of the church, we can also take a look at ourselves and see where we are turning a blind eye to persecution and prejudice in our daily lives and within our communities. We need to regenerate the spiritual ties within our souls—ties to the land, to community, to lovers, to children, to divinity. We cannot do this without the help of our gatekeepers, the two-spirit people, the third-gender folk.

There Is a Way Through

Using the brief overview provided in this chapter, we can hopefully gain an understanding of third-gendered people. They are here and working within society. Some are manifesting their life purpose, but many others, feeling sorrow and abandonment because of cultural rejection, are drifting. To those people I would like to say, "We need you. The Earth needs all her people to fulfill their spiritual purpose and manifest their spiritual gifts into the world."

Within the third-gender archetype resides a spiritual gift for the community. Whether we call them two-spirit people, a he-she, gatekeepers, male-identified females, female-identified males, gays, or lesbians, we do well to keep in mind that they are here on Earth to accomplish a service we so desperately need. We must cross this gender barrier into a greater unity. The indigenous communities have a spiritual tradition and a highly developed language around this gift; we in the West could learn from this teaching.

It may take the resurrection of native and indigenous roles to save us from the gender-war diatribe in which we are engaged. In order to do this we must reeducate ourselves. We must work with the gender diversity we see all around us by helping others (or ourselves) toward greater understanding of our life purpose within this third-gender concept. The gay bashing that is going on is done primarily by white males. This must stop. If we have sexual shadow material manifesting as homophobic tendencies, then we need to work on our shadow regarding our own sexual wounds.

In order for us to effectively change our psychological and sexual ideas, we need an education that combines spirituality with our sexuality and includes third-gender people. By bringing back the spirit into sex, as it once was, we can restructure our relationships, our community, our culture, and the world. Our educational systems must be based in fairness and diversity, endorsing the cultural differences between peoples and traditions. Thus we can overcome the destructive domination and repressive sexual forces that have been imposed on us.

It is within education and self-realization that we will find our freedom and claim our sovereignty. It is through our connection to the spiritual worlds that we can regenerate and gain an understanding of our life purpose. There is a way through our historical and religious repressive tactics. The way is through love and spiritual connection. Through your conscious connection with the spiritual beings, as a man, woman, or two-spirit person, you will learn of your life purpose. You can then go out into the world and help other people who are waiting for you and your gifts.

Divine Conjunctio

Within our Greek myths we have the hermaphrodite who sprang from Hermes, the divine messenger, and Aphrodite, the Goddess of love. In the alchemical union of the male and female, the sun and moon produced the divine androgyne. This combination of male and female is the much-sought-after alchemical Conjunctio—the sacred marriage—where the opposites within our nature synergize into something greater than the separate parts.

Within the creation myth of Genesis, we find that woman and man were one, combined within one body, a symbol of spiritual perfection. Woman and man were split apart to enter separate bodies. Christ has been called the divine androgyne.

Mircea Eliade in his book, *The Two in One,* quotes from an early Christian mystical text, the Gospel of Thomas. In the Gospel of Thomas Jesus said, in an address to the disciples: "And when you make the inner as the outer, and the outer as the inner, and the upper as the lower, and when you make male and female into a single one, so that the male shall not be male and the female (shall not) be female, then shall you enter (the Kingdom)." (p. 106; parenthetical phrases by Eliade)

If we see the blending of the male and female within the framework of our religion, our creation stories, our ancient Greek myths, our Western mystery traditions, Native American and indigenous traditions as well, as a spiritual reality it might behoove us to contemplate this third gender as a positive, ambiguous, paradoxical, mysterious benefit. And noticing the prestigious company it keeps, we might begin to draw the conclusion that our discomfort regarding gender diversity is, simply, our stuff.

Chapter Thirteen

Gender Reconciliation: The Healing Work of Women and Men

    We have separated our lives into isolated compartments. We have made little boxes, each with its own title. This is my relationship. This is my job. This is my home. This is my sexual life. This is my health. This is my dream life. This is my wound. This is my spiritual path. This is my creativity.

    We have also split up men's and women's work into the "women's movement" and the "men's" movement. Within these movements much emotional release and grief work have been done. This separate work is absolutely necessary and critical to healing individual soul wounds as well as the wounds we have inflicted within our own gender groups.

    Men are socialized to be leaders and winner's. To do this they must form hierarchies' and "beat their opponents." Within this competitive construct many men have betrayed their brother in love relationships or in the workplace. This same issue holds true for women as well. Some women may think little of betraying another woman, especially if a man is involved. The sisterhood is not a concept taught as vital character development.

But the separateness of the women and the men also delineates the long entrenched lines of demarcation into two opposing camps-us and them. Between the male and female tensions' lies the wounds that will not heal. If we are to solve our complex problems on a national and world level, we have to first start face to face with individuals, men and women, by addressing directly the wounds between us.

The Blame Game

Some of the feedback from both men's and women's circles and retreats are that the group discussions may (sometimes) dissolve into gripe sessions of blaming the *Other*-either women or men-for the problems or troubles. I realize this is a volatile topic, and I know that gender bashing does not happen in all men's or women's groups. This is a two-way dynamic, and in either case it gets us nowhere.

When we discuss our woundings within the context of men's or women's groups, we have to drop into the details of our story—where we got wounded and who did it to us. Sharing our grief within a safe space brings us out of our isolation. But if we (group leaders and participants) allow derogatory gender bashing to continue unchecked, it will not be particularly healing for anyone involved. It just exaggerates the points of contention between men and women.

Men or women who participate in this blame game may feel better after having vented their feelings within a group format, but they typically go home to their lover after a workshop or class feeling self-righteous, condescending, and patronizing. This can and does lead to distancing communication with their partners. Within this dynamic is the old "us and them" gender war game. This does not promote deep communication or intimacy in the couple or in other relationships. It only underlines a tendency to act superior and generates arguments at home.

What Is the Next Step for Men and Women?

No matter how many revelations or "aha" experiences we have, we are still sitting in separate circles when men and women meet in single-gender groups. I think we may be at a point where we can continue our separate circles but widen our horizons and diversity. I am suggesting another possibility: that men and women who are interested in opening up a mutual dialogue create a third movement—combined men's and women's groups. By addressing our differences in a sacred context, *together,* we will take the next step forward in creating a healthier masculine-feminine paradigm.

A new paradigm shift is calling out to us to stretch beyond the gender split and seek healing for all people before it is too late. How can we facilitate the healing between men and women other than by addressing it directly? We need men and women who are willing to enter this breach and create a space necessary for this kind of realignment work to be done.

It is not enough to have an intellectual grasp of the gender split and to agree with equal rights. Since when has thinking of food actually put food in our mouths? How can it be enough to get somewhat educated about our gender problems and leave it at that? We must take the critical next step of putting our beliefs into *action*. Women and men who are willing to take this leap can gather together in groups and address the issues between them.

We are actually working with an ancient, global thought-form that must be broken down and reformed into a healthy paradigm for all concerned. Incorporating a spiritual framework will call in the help of the spiritual beings and this changes the depth and level of the work dramatically. There may be conflicts during this reformation. Sitting through the conflict-resolution fires, we reach a point where we can see each other as souls housed within human bodies that just happen to be male or female forms. We can see without judgment or blame and wish the best for each other; then we become humans with truly loving hearts.

Dreaming Together

Usually, as the work progresses, the men's and women's circles will start dreaming together. This is very instructive, as the dreams are often prophetic in nature and have proven to be extremely accurate. For example, one of the men had a dream about one of the women in the group. In his dream he was shown a man who was scared and hiding something from this woman. The woman did not know who the person was, but a few months later she found out that her ex-boyfriend (who wanted to be back into her life) had been hiding an affair.

Another woman dreamed about a man in the group and a counselor he was considering working with. The dream information indicated that the counselor was unethical. The man listened to the dream information, took it as precautionary, and decided to proceed with the counselor carefully. Within a very short time the man found the counselor to be, as the dream warned, unethical and he discontinued seeing this counselor.

When the dreaming starts to happen, people are "blown away." Even though they are committed to an intensive spiritual discipline, they are still very surprised when something synchronistic happens to them personally.

The spirits send these dreams to other people in the circle to show how group reciprocity can work and to demonstrate that shamanic dreaming is a reliable information system.

Women and Men in Sacred Space

To get to know men or women in sacred space is an eye-opening experience. Sitting in a circles that are specifically dedicated to healing the breach between genders brings us back into connection with each other and will change the way we typically think in stereotypes. Over time the men and women bond and see each other as individuals, each with their wounds and their gifts, instead of seeing them as *Other*. The field that is woven from the group work is beautiful to experience as we sit next to one another and begin our descent into the story.

The women and men share intimate stories that directly address scenarios of abusive power and gender relations. A mom who beats her son. A father who sexually molested his daughter. A women who was pregnant, got an abortion, and was abandoned by her lover. A man whose father beat him senseless; a mother who molested her little boy; parents who gave enemas, beatings, or rapes as daily or weekly occurrences.

These stories are shocking, moving and painful. It is especially so when one of the women comes to circle to share she was just date-raped. Men sitting in circle as sacred witnesses, listening to a woman who has entered their hearts as one of their sisters tell how she was raped by a man who asked her out on a date—this is a deep-felt teaching. It brings the women's issues from the abstract to the individual. They listen to her share her account of saying no, of being hit and thrown down and threatened with her life. How she kicked him, spit in his face, how he hit her again and raped her as her spirit flew from her body.

Women have just as powerful an experience of compassion and understanding of the *Other* when they listen to the story of a man's pain while moving into fatherhood, or how he survived the sexual abuse by his mother, or the shame and brutality of high-school hazing from other boys. These tales provide the necessary ingredient to show women that, indeed, men do not have the world served up to them on a silver platter.

This work heals the male-female wound within us, our families, and the human community as we take this knowledge with us into our regular lives. We see men and women all around us differently, for it has been revealed to us in circle that we are all connected as brothers and sisters. We are all trying to find love and acceptance.

But the Work is not just for releasing grief, telling our stories or understanding our internalized family patterns. It is to bring the men and women together into sacred space and to develop rituals of forgiveness, grief, healing, renewal and reconciliation between the sacred Feminine and sacred Masculine. May it be So.

Chapter Fourteen

Creativity: The Lost Arts

Spiritual Disconnection

Creativity—the original act of making, of expressing—invokes divine forces that may appear to us as ideas, emotions, potency, passion, longing, yearning, melancholy, enthusiasm, ecstasy, joy, love, hurt, pain, or desire. Creativity means to work with an inner force that wants to be ex-pressed outwardly into some form. We do not have an understanding of the critical importance of the arts in relation to the health of soul and hence to the nation.

The new physics informs us that "something else" is out there. The universe is made of "stuff" that is malleable and flexible; it moves and forms in relation to our thoughts and will force. This only means that we now understand we were not looking correctly in order to perceive this reality. This "new" reality has always been here. We are just now "scientifically" proving what has been stated for centuries by mystics, shamans, and dreamers in ancient literature and holy texts.

If the stuff of the universe interacts with our will-directed thinking and forms itself with some plasticity and elasticity according to those thought forms, then we are dealing with stuff that responds to and interacts with us. This brings us back full circle to the importance and impact of character development and by a longer loop to the artist.

People who have the capacity to work with the universal material are what we would call sensitives and creators—people who can place their awareness outside themselves, bring it back, and create into some form what they witnessed or understood. These people tend to live on the borders of society. Who lives on the outer rim, the boundaries of cultural form? Who are the people who have not, will not conform to social stratification? Think about it. It may be you.

The Artist Is Dreaming the Future of Evolution

These people have generally been grouped in the category of "artist types." These are the folks who are better equipped because they have not let go of their inner soul connection to the universe of the unseen. These are the edge-walkers; they stand in liminal space on the borders of conformity, social norms, and the great beyond.

It is within these soul types that we will discover the ones who are working with birthing the new evolutionary forces onto the planet. Many of these people are fully aware of the extraordinary changes and have worked hand in hand with the angelic realms in order to keep us alive. Many incarnated into life directions that would directly address and assist our evolutionary leap. Keeping the label of "artist types" to include mystics, healers, and dreamers as well as artists will allow us to witness the gift they bring to our communities and to the world.

Artists, because they stand at the edges, can see farther than the ordinary mortal. They are not as rigidly constructed as most folks are (especially here in the Western world) and their feeling nature is highly developed. This means they are extremely sensitive to the fluctuations and energy surges of the universe-in-making. This allows them to stretch their antenna, if you will, out into the web of our universal weaving. They bring back ingenious designs, inventions, and ideas that will help anchor the new energy of the evolutionary dynamic once it manifests.

With this kind of skill and life purpose we can see that character development of the creator-artist would be the integral measure with which to weigh the merit of the inspired designs coming in from the borderlands of the Earth and spiritual planes. The clearer the vessel, the clearer the energy. To become a clear vessel takes many lifetimes of discipline and dedication to an initiate's path of self-sacrifice.

There are many such beings who will never be recognized for their service to humanity's needs. Artists are essential all over the globe to anchor inspired work, whether or not their names become known. This ability to work with the unseen spiritual worlds in relation to the arts is a blessed gift and service to the planet.

The Hidden Messages within Art

The arts in different cultures vary greatly because each person has a particular gift they are bringing to the Earth. And within each culture individuals will work with many spirits that wish to be in-formed. The Hopi believe that if they do not perform their creative rituals the world will dissolve. Looking all over the world into the diverse cultures, we see raw primary colors, ragged edges, carved wood, wrapped bones, ceramic pottery, exquisite icons, beaded jewelry, mosaics of marble, blown glass, primal sculpture, and gold-leaf ceilings—all representations of inner symbols and voyages.

People create art for many different reasons. If we want to invoke a feeling of divinity within the viewer, we will use images, symbols, gestures, colors to invite that experience. If we want to make an art piece that is healing or holds power, we will infuse our ideas with that power and move it into the art. If we want to make a piece to express some strong emotions or to say the unsayable, art is the flexible, moldable, movable, carveable, additive or subtractive medium. And within that medium are hundreds of forms, including paper, wood, canvas, furniture, cloth, music, dance, theater, sculpture. Anything goes.

So much of our world is based on action: doing, accomplishing, manifesting something for some reason. We go to work in order to "make" money, in order to pay for housing and food. Creating art is also an action, but it is an action that can connect the heart, soul, and spirit of an individual. Art is en-souled action. When we create, we can connect to our deep selves. In the artistic process we can lose a sense of our "I-ness" and relax or surrender to a greater spirit. To create or play in an artistic process rejuvenates our spirit. Not only do we transform the materials with which we work but we transform ourselves as well.

Often the next step in this creation process sends the art out into the world in some form, and that transforms the viewers. The art carries a message within itself. The work of artists who are bringing into form the evolutionary energies will call forth that response within the individuals who see it. This response can be conscious or unconscious for the viewer; nonetheless, the seed is planted and a reawakening is gestating within the soul.

The Art Wound

I believe that everyone is an artist. There are no right or wrong ways to paint, sculpt, play, carve, dance, or write. There are "accepted" ways and forms, but that does not mean they are "right." There is no correct way to create. Having said that, I know that many, many folks have been mortally wounded at some point when they were engrossed and inspired in an art project. Just at the point where your soul was soaring with delight, someone told you that you could not paint the trees purple or that squiggle was not a girl, or that certainly doesn't look like a monkey.

Or worse yet, they saw you had talent and tried to squash you so you would not follow or develop it. They do this because they are shadow artists—"once-upon-a-time artists" who gave up on themselves long ago. Or maybe they don't want you to be a bohemian, flaky artist type. They want you to be a doctor or an engineer. Or maybe they were just plain mean.

In either case, you picked up on their "squash-'em" energy. Their dart reached your heart, and suddenly your fantastic creation deflated into something scarred and worthless. But *they* did not do that to you; you bought the lie. You could have turned to them and said, "get-lost." But we buy the lie, usually because we are young. Typically this squashing happens when we are children. We are young and we believe *they* know better than us.

To tell someone that they are not an artist is heartless and cruel. But we do eventually grow out of the range of intimidation and control. Why do we not pick up that pencil and continue? Because deep down we are afraid they are right. We can even prove this to ourselves by comparing our work to the "greats" of our day. Often we do not pick up the pencil or paints ever again. We let our artistic surges go unanswered until we forget what an artistic impulse feels like. After some years we do not give it another thought.

We do not just lose our artistic inspirations. That creation energy goes somewhere. Where is it going? It can be re-channeled in healthy ways or unhealthy ways. The loss of the inspiration to create is often sublimated with something else, either another creative outlet or such activities as doing drugs, having sex, shopping, eating, reading, watching videos.

When I was in high school I would go on fabric-buying binges. I would come home with armloads of fabrics in violets, teal blues, maroons, floral prints, silks, weaves, cottons. When I started buying enormous amounts of fabric to design and sew outfits, my mother used to say to me, "Kristena, you need to be painting with color. Your soul longs for color." Once when I had the urge to buy different kinds of fabrics, I tried what she suggested. I painted a painting instead. I worked in color. You know what? She was right. After working in the realm of color I did not want to sew five outfits.

The Artist's Wound is a Loss of Soul

If our first creative outflow was put down or suppressed, we probably suffered humiliation and great embarrassment. If we were traumatized by the disparagement of our creativity, then some part of our soul left during the wounding. I would like to say that any soul loss resulting from other kinds of trauma will affect our creativity as well. But within this chapter I am concentrating only on the art wound. Many depressed and blocked creative people, as well as people who call themselves "wounded artists," are suffering from soul loss due to an art wound. Soul retrieval is a wonderful healing to bring back that artful soul piece that fled the body due to shock or shame.

Suffering soul loss around an art wound is very common. The stories I hear from men and women about how their artistic fountain ran dry or was shut off are truly disheartening. Soul loss from an art wound is just like soul loss from any other trauma—wounds are wounds. And that soul part will have to come back into your body in order for you to have your spiritual essence and your artistic sense.

Spontaneous soul retrieval is a possibility. Some people take in-depth workshops on recovering creativity and have transforming experiences around their creativity. Their soul part comes back. From that point on they are imbued with the ebb and flow of creativity again. You know you've had a spontaneous soul retrieval around your art wound if you begin playing with art again, on a continuing basis.

I have developed weekend workshops for soul-retrieval healing in the areas of art. The days are filled with circle sharing about each person's wound, how it affected them and what consequences they experienced. Participants paint pictures, sing songs, and perform dances to show how and where the wound landed in the body-scape. The group receives a soul retrieval and the rest of the time is spent in creating rituals with sacred art.

A Call to Our Creative Powers

If you don't have access to a shamanic practitioner, the next best thing for healing your art wound is to do a journey yourself and find an art teacher. Looking at all the diverse traditions, we can see that art is a form of worship. Many shamans' spirit helpers informed, taught, instructed, and guided the shaman in the color, form, and design of a shamanic art piece. The spirits also taught the shaman how to empower the art to make it sacred for use in ceremony.

The journeys described below can help you contact your own spirit teacher of the sacred arts. You can request the teacher to help you call back your creative powers and perhaps your soul. Remember, these teachers possess great powers and abilities. They are like vast warehouses of ancient secrets embodied in the arts.

Journey to Find a Sacred Art Teacher 15min

Follow the general outline for journeying as described in previous chapters. I suggest that you journey for 15 minutes to find a sacred art teacher. The teacher may be a power animal or a human being. Be open to whoever comes for you. Your intention is to find a teacher who will instruct you in the sacred arts.

Go to your departure place and state your intention. Follow who comes for you—if your power animal takes you to the lower world, follow them. If an upper-world teacher takes you up, follow them. Ask them to introduce you to an instructor of the sacred arts. When you meet the sacred art teacher (who may be a teacher you already know and love), ask them how they will work with you and what they would like in return. If they take you somewhere, pay attention. When you hear the drumming call-back on the tape, remember to use the entire time to re-enter your body fully.

Journey to Ask Your Sacred Art Teacher

for a Ceremonial Art Piece 20min

In this second journey you are going back to your teacher of sacred art. The 20-minute journey has two parts:

A. When you meet your art teacher, ask whether you lost soul in relation to creativity. Ask them to show you when it happened.

B. Ask the teacher to give you an idea for an art piece that you will make to call back your creative power and your soul. This part of the journey has five aspects.

Request an image for an art piece to make to call back your creative soul.
Or you could request an art piece to symbolize the negative internalizing of your creative spirit--this piece you would destroy, burn or bury. Please make out of natural objects!
Look at how the art is made. How is it designed?
What materials is it made of?
Ask your teacher how to empower the art piece.
The teacher will give you a technique or ritual of empowerment. When you perform that ritual with the art piece, the art will become a house for the power of your teacher to reside in. This is how you will receive the healing.

Ask your teacher what you are do with the art piece. Keep it, burn it, bury it, hang it?

When you hear the drumming call-back, remember to use the entire time to re-enter your body fully. Write down your journey and what you learned. Did you lose soul in relation to your creativity? Draw your art object, adding all the details you saw—color, materials, design, size, shape—everything. Write down the ritual of empowerment. Then create what the teacher showed you, do your ritual of empowerment, and carry out the final outcome for the art piece.

Personal Totem: Manifesting Soul Essence

Now we get to the fun and wildly creative part. If you have used this book as a learning manual for esoteric teachings, taken up your dream journal, and used it as your personal workbook, then you have taken a voyage through your soul consciousness—your thinking, feeling, and willing; your body, mind, and spirit. You may have discovered much about yourself that perhaps delighted you, dismayed you, and surprised you. Hopefully you have had some successful journeys and discovered your allies and helping spirits.

The last exercise of this book is to create a personal totem or icon that represents your manifested self. By combining all you have learned and what it is you want in your life purpose, vocation, beloved, sexuality, health, creativity, and spirituality, you can come up with some wonderful design and make it for yourself.

You can use any media—clay, wood, paper, paint, pencils, crayons—and make a doll, painting, or sculpture. I would ask that you create a physical, hands-on object rather than writing a poem, song, story, etc. It's fine to include that verbal side, but this experience is mostly designed to ground you in the act of creating with your hands an object that will empower you and call you toward your intended self.

What will it be? What will it look like? How will you design it? You can journey to your art teacher and co-create an art piece or you can dive right in and begin, following your intuition. To begin, consider what you learned with every topic you've explored.

What do you want from relationship?
What do you want from creativity?
What do you want in your sexual life?
What do you want for your vocation or life purpose?
What do you want for your spiritual life?
What do you want for your health?

Now, how can you translate those hopes and dreams into a form? Would it be abstract or representational? An altar? A cloth doll? A small clay sculpture? A dancing figure? An animal? Go to it. Please don't get caught up in doubt—

just gather your materials and dive in, make a mess, create chaos, and allow mistakes to lead you deeper into the process. Allow your "young self" to have some fun—let your imagination roam, go to extremes, create from your heart on a whim.

Invite the spirits to play with you. Ask them to help you call your soul into manifestation. You will be surprised how much help you get from them. Perhaps you have already had a dream while reading this book that urges you to re-create it. Listen to that dream... it is calling you. When you've completed your totem, you can perform a ritual of empowerment and call on the help of your allies and teachers, making this artwork your own personal power piece.

If you have some struggle, go through it. Grow through it. Don't let it stop or hinder your outflow of creative juices. Creation is a birth process, and part of that process is the tension or struggle to release the sacred art you feel within your soul. Let it flow through your body and mind. Allow the power and potency of pure, raw creativity to lay new pathways within your soul being. You can journey for a ritual of empowerment. Good luck and have fun!

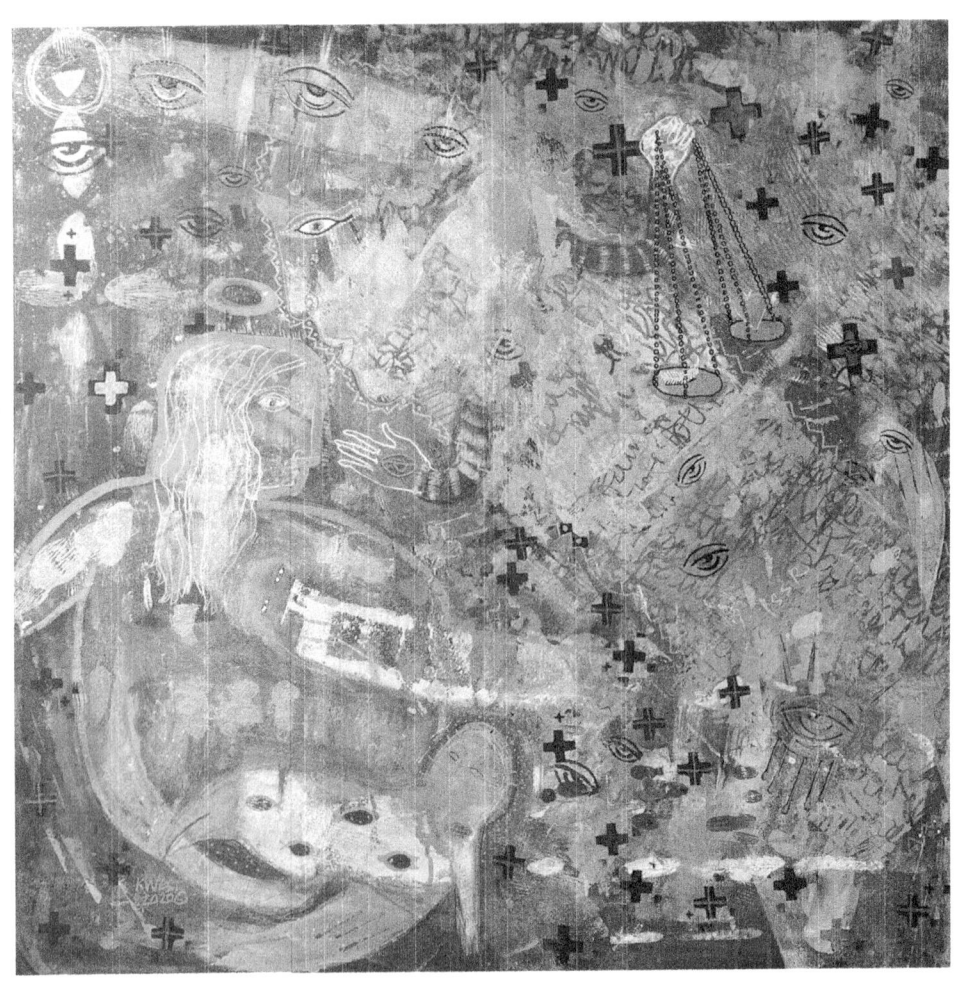

Michael and Maat: Weighing the Heart
Kristena West 2020

Bibliography

Alchemy
Jung, C.J. *Alchemy a Western Mystery Tradition*
Jung, C.J. *Psychology & Alchemy*
von Franz, Marie-Louise. *Alchemy*

Alternative Healing
Brennen, Barbara Ann. *Hands of Light*
Brennen, Barbara Ann. *Light Emerging*
Myss, Caroline Ph.D. *Anatomy of the Spirit*
Weiss, Brian M.D. *Through Time Into Healing*

Ceremony, Magic & Ritual
Noble, Vicki. *Shakti Woman: New Female Shamanism*
StarHawk. *The Spiral Dance*

Dream Work
Barasch, Marc Ian. *Healing Dreams; Exploring Dreams that can Transform Your Life*
Castaneda, Carlos. *The Art of Dreaming*
Delany, Dr. Delany. *Break Through Dreaming*
Garfield, Patricia Ph.D. *Creative Dreaming*
Guiley, Rosemary Ellen. *Dreamwork for the Soul*
Johnson, Robert. *Balancing Heaven & Earth*

La Berge, Stephen. *Lucid Dreaming*
Jung, C.J. *Memories, Dreams & Reflections*
Monroe, Robert. *Journey's Out of the Body*
Monroe, Robert. *Far Journeys, Ultimate Journey*
Moss, Robert. *Conscious Dreaming*
Steiner, Rudolf. *Occult Science.*

Gender
Jacobs, Sue-Ellen & Thomas, Wesley & Lang, Sabine. *Two-Spirit People*
Roscoe, Will. *Changing Ones*
Williams, Walter. *The Spirit and the Flesh*
Herr Van Nostrand, Catherine. *Gender Responsible Leadership*

Kundalini
Krishna, Gopi. *Kundalini, Kundalini Rising*
St.Romain, Philip. *Kundalini Energy and Christian Spirituality*
Kornfield, Jack. *After the Ecstasy, the Laundry; How the Heart Grows Wise on the Spiritual Path.*

Relationship & Spirituality

Bradshaw, John. *Creating Love*
Lee, John. *The Flying Boy*
Levine, Steven. *Embracing the Beloved*
Pederson, Loren. Dark Hearts: Unconscious Forces That Shape Men's Lives
Silbury, Lira. *The Sacred Marriage*
Tannen Ph.D., Deborah. *You Just Don't Understand*
Zukov, Gary. *Seat of the Soul*
Zweig, Connie. *Embracing the Shadow*

Sexuality

Carnes Ph.D., Patrick. *Don't Call it Love*
Carnes Ph.D., Patrick. *Out of the Shadows*
Lawlor, Robert. *Earth Honoring: The New Male Sexuality*
Sipe, Richard. A Secret World, Sex, Priests & Power
Wilson Shaef, Anne. *Escape from Intimacy*

Shamanism

Harner, Michael. *The Way of the Shaman*
Ingerman, Sandra. *Soul Retrieval & Welcome Home*
Kalweit, Holger. *Dreamtime & Inner Space*
Cowan, Tom. *Shamanism: A Spiritual Practice for Everyday Life*

Prechtel, Martin. *Honey in the Heart, Secrets of the Talking Jaguar*

Western Mystery Traditions
Steiner, Rudolf. *How to Attain Knowledge of the Higher Worlds*
Steiner, Rudolf. *A Western Approach to Reincarnation and Karma*
Matthews, John. *Celtic Shamanism*
Fortune, Dion. *The Mystical Kabbalah*
Fortune, Dion. *Training & Work of an Initiate*

Women's Studies
Achterberg, Jeanne. *Woman as Healer*
Barstow, Anne. *Witchcraze*
Eisler, Riane. *Sacred Pleasure: Sex, Myth & the Politics of the Body*
Kramer, Heinrich. *The Malleus Maleficarum; Dover Books*

Made in the USA
Monee, IL
22 April 2022